—— PATHWAYS TO EX

ORIENTEERING

Published 1994 by

HARVEYS
12-16 Main Street
Doune, Perthshire, FK16 6BJ
Tel: 0786 841202
Fax: 0786 841098

PETER PALMER

Before becoming the British Orienteering Federation's first director of
coaching, Peter Palmer taught in
Secondary Schools of all types for
30 years. He is now a school
governor and member of the
curriculum committee, and is still
active with wife Marlene in developing junior orienteering at national, regional and local levels.

   At various times during the past
twenty years he has chaired BOF
Schools' and Coaching Committees,
founded and organised the National
Junior Squad from which most of
Britain's current crop of orienteers
have emerged, and run national
and international orienteering
courses on junior and grass roots
orienteering development. These
include four International Orienteering Federation "Clinic" in
Sweden, as well as courses for
teachers and coaches in Canada,
Bulgaria, Hong Kong and Australia.
He also has wide experience in
planning and organising major
national championships and international competitions.

   His publications include "The
Coaching Collection" (with Jim
Martland), "Back to Basics", now
translated into Russian, The IOF's
"Orienteering for the Young" (with
Carol McNeill and Tom Renfrew)
and, with Carol and Jim again, the
National Curriculum Guide for Key
Stages 1 & 2, and 3 & 4.

   Peter is pictured on the back
cover with the 1993 men's World
Championship Silver Medal winning relay team.

Pathways to Excellence

Peter Palmer

HARVEYS

Dedication

To Marlene, Mary, Steve - and all those blue remembered forests.

Acknowledgements

Orienteering exists through its wide family of (planners, organisers, mappers and) enthusiasts. I have been guided along so many fascinating paths by these very special people. My thanks go to all those many families, coaches and teachers at home and abroad who have provided motivation and so many ideas.

The Hales, Leijons, Lightfoots, Peels and Bradleys in particular will see some of themselves in this book. So will Martin Bagness, Dave Gittus and Carol McNeill who have provided drawings and illustrations as well as inspiration. The world of orienteering, like this book, owes them all an enormous debt for their dedication and hard work.

My thanks also go to Sue Harvey for her encouragement to write the book and tireless proof-reading, and Robin for design work and wise advice.

Thanks also to clubs and schools for permission to use map extracts and to Silva UK Ltd for compass bearing illustration.

Cartoons drawn by Martin Bagness.

Photos by Ken Price, Jonathan Taylor and David Briggs.

Contents

Introduction

Orienteering does not lend itself to simple definitions. It combines navigation, running, problem-solving, challenge and the aesthetic appeal of countryside environments. It appeals to a wide variety of tastes, interests and sensibilities. It can take many forms: cross-country orienteering, score orienteering, night orienteering, sprint orienteering, mountain orienteering, trail-orienteering, mountain bike orienteering, ski orienteering, community orienteering or a rogaine; it can take place in many different natural settings and demand varying levels of technical and physical skills. Essentially however, there is a common core to all these activities, the challenge of completing a testing navigational course relying on skills of map and compass plus a dash of determination and cunning.

In Britain especially, orienteering has evolved into the ultimate family sport in which parents and children can either compete individually on courses specially designed for their personal levels of age and experience, or take part recreationally as a group. It is also a sport run by participants for participants. While there are professionals in the field, on the whole orienteers make their own maps, plan their own courses and organise their own events. Like every sport, if it is to be truly enjoyed, it demands a mastery of certain basic skills, but these are simple to learn and develop. From the very first steps, introductory courses in school grounds or city parks can open up areas of exploration experience. Skills learned in the small scale can then be put to the test in the wider outdoors of forest, mountain or moor.

British orienteering in its early days followed a rambling path in which coaching and systematic learning of skills did not play a significant part. The early pioneers of the late 60's and early 70's emerged from a running, rambling or outdoor activity background, bringing a rudimentary knowledge of Ordnance Survey maps, a stoical determination not to be defeated by the inadequacies of inaccurate maps and an optimistic will to triumph over every challenge and hardship. In these 'prehistoric' orienteering events survival was all. There was little attention to technique and training methods.

I was very much part of this scene, and, in a sense, my personal performance has never recovered from it. However, thirty years of growing up with a new sport, of learning from mistakes in planning and organisation, and helping to build a British Coaching structure has not only provided me with a rich vein of experience, but also, I hope, the capacity to see the learning process through a beginner's eyes. I have the same love-hate relationship with orienteering as with skiing - a dynamic tension between "the better you do something the more you enjoy it" philosophy and the "why do I always make mistakes through doing things I know to be wrong" sense of frustration.

My first coaching experience was with school pupils on Surrey Common for whom orienteering provided a more interesting experience for 'thinking runners' than simple cross-country runs. Since those early days in the 60's I have worked with a school-based club on Cannock Chase, the West Mid-

Punching at a control

lands and National Junior Squads, and from 1985 to 1992 with orienteers of all ages and abilities in my work as Director of Coaching in the British Orienteering Federation. My wife Marlene has always provided a vital woman's perspective as well as dedicated work in the coaching cause, and both my children have grown up in the sport. My son, Stephen, as top international competitor, World Championship medallist and elite coach, gives a progressive insight into training demands and coaching theories at the top, while my work with other national coaches in Australia, Canada, the USA, SE Asia and all corners of Europe has not only given me many ideas on effective ways of coaching skills and developing the sport, but strengthened my belief that orienteering can be adapted to practically any environment and that the same basic skills, if taught well, work everywhere.

To Sweden I owe a particular debt. Without the help and ideas freely provided by a series of inspiring teachers and coaches, the maps, forests and club huts provided for our training camps and the annual coaching clinics run in conjunction with the O-Ringen, Sweden's International 5 Days Competition, so much exciting development work would not have been possible.

In the pages which follow I have tried to distil my experience into a progressive programme for working on orienteering skills and using effective methods of teaching and developing them. I first discussed these basic skills in a series of articles entitled "Back to Basics" in the orienteering magazine "Compass Sport". I argued that they would be of interest and assistance to orienteers of every level of ability from school pupil in a local park to the elite competitor in a Scandinavian forest. Although the techniques described here are essentially an orienteering method of navigation they can be applied equally effectively in the wider outdoor world and can readily be adapted to all types of terrain and map. In the same way that the British Orienteering Federation (BOF) coaching ladder (see page 17), can help well motivated orienteers to develop their full potential, so the National Navigational Award Scheme can encourage any walker, climber or fell runner to develop navigational skills and thereby explore the countryside with more confidence and pleasure.

A special feature of this book is that skills acquisition and coaching are tackled in the context of a family taking up the sport and progressing fitfully

Never too young to learn

through its various dimensions. The Wood family is fictional, but its introduction to orienteering and the progress of its individual members are rooted in fact. Their first encounter with a Forestry Permanent Course, the children's experiences in school and their first attempts in BOF competitions will be familiar to many active orienteers, and by examining their performances and expectations, the reader can appreciate more readily the relevance of skills training in enhancing enjoyment as well as the opportunities which exist to help orienteers of all ages and abilities get more from a fascinating sport. I hope this gives skills coaching and the attendant training exercises which accompany each chapter a keener cutting edge.

It's time to set off now with our friends, the Wood family, on the first stage of their orienteering journey. I hope with them we can share some of the thrill which David Livingstone must have felt on first setting eyes on Lake Victoria or Neil Armstrong on stepping on the Moon. Essentially, all orienteering is an adventure, but any successful exploration relies on confidence, planning, the application of navigational skills and attention to safety. Getting lost can never be a positive experience.

If this book encourages its readers to tackle the orienteering scene in this spirit then the writing of it will have been worthwhile. Like the Woods, you may well find that the orienteering trail takes some strange twists and turns and that the outcome isn't always what was expected, but unlike Columbus, at least you will know where you're going, where you've been and the most effective way of reaching places you want to go to next time - not a bad recipe for life really .... but then, orienteering is a way of life as much as a sport.

1 First steps

This way, shouted the boy. "Come on Dad: it's up this path". Off he sprinted through the tall pine trees, the needles underfoot muffling his steps, as he made for a small totem pole crowned with a red and white prism and emblazened with a large letter 'R' in black.

Behind him straggled a bizarre queue - a heavy balding man clutching a map, a young girl trying to disguise any connection with the whole undignified proceedings and mother attempting to interest a tearful small daughter in a startled squirrel as they perspired up the slope towards "Hawkeye the Pathfinder" now proclaiming to the whole world from the top of the knoll that "he'd found it".

"Can we go back now", wailed Natalie, pulling her mother towards the path which pointed invitingly downhill towards the Forestry Office they'd left half an hour earlier.

"Don't be a wimp", scoffed older sister, Samantha. "We're half way round and it's mostly downhill now."

"Go on, take her back" was Christopher's helpful contribution before he was off into the trees again grasping his map like a relay baton.

Mother and father looked at one another and then at the map, a colourful creation, entitled Forest Enterprise Permanent Orienteering Course. At first glance its web of paths, streams, marshes and contour lines seemed daunting and the twenty small red circles which ringed a series of tiny features didn't appear to present a coherent pattern or message. As father Michael peered at the red ringed hill contour where they were now standing, which was numbered 3, and then at the circles numbered 4, 5 and 6, he began to wonder whether what had seemed such a good idea an hour ago on the camp site was about to disintegrate into a family endurance test of farcical proportions.

"Mum and Natalie can go back down the path with Patch the dog" he found himself saying. "You can go on, Chris, and I will help Sam and cut off towards the finish if we find we're taking too long."

The recreational spirit in which the Wood family had started off that morning was being distorted by Chris into a more competitive vein. Unwittingly he was moving from wayfaring into orienteering, a much more competitive activity in which a prime trap is outrunning one's technique, as Chris was about to discover - for, as Natalie's voice faded in to the distance and the pine trees grew taller and darker, Chris' headlong charge started to lose its impetus, and then lost Chris himself. Without compass or paths to direct his progress, Chris now stood beside a marsh trying desperately to focus on his crumpled map through a sea of sweat and to come to terms with the twin realisations that he was very lonely and very lost. To make matters worse, his befuddled brain seemed incapable of controlling his wayward legs which inexorably began to take him downhill, away from Control 4, and straight into the arms of his mother who was as surprised as Chris to find themselves together on the path leading back to the camp site.

Fig 1.1: "Here it is,Grandma"

Half an hour later, it was the turn of Dad and Samantha to hit the same path, three controls better off than Christopher, proving another of the adages of orienteering, that the careful tortoise often beats the impetuous hare. Five minutes later, they were proudly flaunting their completed control card to the rest of the family: F - O - R - E - S - T. Six letters collected from the control posts to make up the word which proved they'd finished the course.

That evening, the family sat outside their tent in the last of some Easter sun, licking their wounds and comparing notes on their first experience of orienteering.

"The Forestry Office notice didn't tell you how fit you had to be to get up all those hills", complained Mum.

1	2	3	4	5	6	7	8	9	10	11	12
F	O	R	E	S	T						
13	14	15	16	17	18	19	20	21	22	23	24
25	26	27	28	29	30	31	32	33	34	35	36

	Name:		Finish	•	•	
			Start	•	•	
			Time	•	•	

Fig 1.2: Control card

"The slide-tape introduction made it seem too easy", commented Dad.

"I couldn't understand the complicated map and 1:10,000 scale", pouted Christopher.

"I thought it was great", smirked Samantha. "The best bit was seeing your face, Chris, when we finished."

"I saw the squirrel and fell in a stream", boasted Natalie, "and I liked the ice cream at the end."

Patch made no comment. He was stretched out under the back of the car, fast asleep and no doubt dreaming of a doggy forest paradise full of rabbits and exciting smells.

Like many families, the Woods had tried a Permanent Orienteering Course while on a camping holiday. There are now over 150 Permanent Courses all over Britain, many set up by local authorities in urban parks, though the majority are run by Forest Enterprise. Permanent control points are set out in a forest or park and shown by red circles on a detailed coloured map. This is usually sold at a Visitor Centre or Site Office. A complete package usually involves map, control descriptions and explanation sheet and sometimes includes a list of local orienteering clubs, fixtures and contact addresses. Sequences of controls are suggested to form courses of varying length and difficulty and certificates are often awarded in exchange for completed control cards. Basically, permanent course orienteering offers pleasant

WAYFARING

This is to certify that

....

located .... control points

....

Fig. 1.3: Certificate

woodland walks in which participants choose their own route and speed and via the control points visit the most interesting and attractive parts of the forest. Permanent courses can be used by clubs, groups or schools as well as individuals and can be very useful for setting up small competitions or practising training ideas.

The Woods had set out together to do a 3 kilometre course which visited 6 control points. They had bought only 2 maps which meant that, typically, only two males, Dad and Chris, were involved in the map reading and choice of routes. Their comments after their first experience of orienteering were fairly representative of those made by newcomers to the activity.

Fig 1.4: Bryn-engan: a complicated orienteering map of Welsh mountain terrain adjoining the Plas y Brenin Centre for Mountain Activities.

Most walkers are familiar with conventional maps like those published by the Ordnance Survey at scales of 1:25,000 and 1:50,000 but, like Chris, they can find orienteering maps strange to get used to. These specially produced maps are usually at the large scales of 1:10,000 (approx. 6" to 1 mile) or 1:15, 000. Unlike Ordnance Survey maps the vertical north lines indicate magnetic instead of true or grid north which means that no allowance has to be made in taking compass bearings. There are no numbered grids to provide map references. While some Forest Enterprise wayfaring maps use green to indicate the forested areas, all orienteering maps show open traversable forest as white (uncoloured), which allows other detail to stand out more clearly, green being retained for dense forest where progress is difficult. Various shades of yellow indicate fields and open areas, while brown is used for contour lines and ground features like earth banks, gullies and knolls. Blue is used for water features and black for man-made features like paths, roads and buildings. (A list of symbols used in orienteering maps is shown in appendix I). Although to the practised eye, orienteering maps are clear and easy to read, for newcomers the prominence given to small contour detail and point features like boulders and depressions can be confusing at first.

Mum, or Helen as we'll now call her, was right to bring up the issue of fitness. Although there are now computer games which simulate wayfaring and orienteering, and armchair map reading can be absorbing, one of the essential elements of orienteering is exploring the countryside and discovering the secrets of real forests. It goes without saying that woodland and heathland are rarely flat or obstruction free and that even walking along paths requires a basic level of fitness. The casual orienteer doesn't have to be a trained athlete but does need to enjoy walking and the conquest of tiredness. Orienteering in full sport mode raises the physical element another notch, for, whether taking things steadily without navigational mistakes like Samantha, or running round paths like Christopher, the fastest wins and 'fast' usually means running. For orienteering, the description Cunning Running (or walking) is probably better than "The Thought Sport'.

Michael (father in the Wood household) had commented on difficulty. Orienteering, like route finding in the car or navigating a yacht across the channel, requires mastery of basic skills which then have to be fitted together into a practised sequence, like using words in a sentence when writing.

Nor were Natalie's thoughts irrelevant. Orienteering is about the natural world, wet feet and the social 'goodies' afterwards - as well as finding the best routes, discovering the control markers, walking or running along soft pine needle paths and negotiating spectacular ridges.

Orienteering can be recreational or competitive navigation. Both cover a variety of sins, as the Wood family had already discovered.

For the Woods however, and for us, the story is only just beginning. Just as they had started the orienteering course together and then proceeded to interpret its challenges in their own ways, so their choice of routes in following up the experience and exploiting different dimensions of the orienteering idea were to be personal to themselves and their own experience, though still tackled within a family perspective.

This is the story this book now follows. The Woods could be any family; the experiences described here are all based upon fact. The exercises suggested for developing their interest are all well tried. Put simply, it is a blow by blow, unvarnished account of a family's attempts to take up a new absorbing activity and to succeed in it at each member's personal level. In the process, they come to realise that orienteering, like every sport, has skills which have to be learnt and practised. They also learn to cope with disappointment, as well as enjoying the rich satisfaction of achievement, and as the highs exceed the lows both in number and intensity so they are drawn further on to make themselves even better and to extend the bounds of their experience.

The skills sections which form the second half of each chapter are vital to its message. They give the book a very special dimension which make it much more than an armchair read. Each section catalogues skills, ideas and training exercises relevant to the preceding narrative. Some will want to skim these sections on the first reading and refer back to them at a later date.

I want you to enjoy sharing the Woods' experiences. I would like you to follow them. Much more than that, I hope that by reading my recipe for improving orienteering performance you will not only give orienteering a try (if you haven't done so already) but also that your enjoyment from it will be that much deeper and more varied.

Fig. 1.5: Success in the early stages is vital: setting his map and concentrating like this and he'll achieve it

Skills for getting started

In one sense, the Wood family's introduction to orienteering, though a familiar one, was not ideal. Unstructured Permanent Course Orienteering in which competitors choose a sequence of controls at random can produce navigational problems which are usually avoided in planning a beginners' course, where the course-setter intentionally avoids hazards like marshes or brambly thickets and keeps beginners' to paths and tracks. Even short cross-country stretches require compass skills, and

Learning Orienteering Step By Step

LEVEL 6 — Difficult control points.
Pacing.
Longer legs and longer distances to catching features and attack points.

LEVEL 5 — Using the correct technique with changes in difficulty. Reading contours at competition speed. Using check points to pinpoint position.

LEVEL 4 — Reading contours in detail. Orienteering using large knolls, significant re-entrants, and ridges.

LEVEL 3 — Fine orienteering on short legs. Rough orienteering on longer legs against catching features. Relocation techniques. Making simple route choices. Using contour lines to picture simple ground shapes.

LEVEL 2 — Orienteering on short legs against catching features. Shortcuts using compass bearings and distance judgement. Reading objects by paths. Taking controls just off paths using attack points.

LEVEL 1 — Orienteering from path to path. Orienteering along a single path and using other "lines" as handrails. Map colours, and most commonly used symbols. Orientating the map using terrain and compass.

GROUND LEVEL — Understanding the map. Orientating the map. Getting used to being in the woods.

Fig 1.6: Skills step ladder

missing a control can easily translate into getting hopelessly lost, as Chris quickly discovered.

So what basic skills did the Woods need before having their first go at orienteering, and what in an ideal world would have made the best introduction? On the previous page we show the Skills Step Ladder which all orienteers should attempt to climb systematically if they wish to acquire a competent grasp of the sport. It was first devised in Sweden and has been adapted to British experience. (Sweden, with a long history of orienteering dating back to the end of the last century, is one of the strongest orienteering nations in the world, and has developed some of the most effective strategies for introducing the sport to newcomers both inside and outside the school curriculum. References to Swedish experience are frequent throughout the text.)

If each skill is learnt and practised in turn, starting at the bottom, then the average orienteer should be able to compete as confidently as a club golfer or tennis player who has had a series of lessons from a professional. This should give confidence so that, even if winning is not on the cards, at least there are going to be no traumatic disasters. Getting lost is orienteering's biggest turn-off. One Swedish teacher commented to me "I don't like getting lost, and neither do my pupils. Using a map, a compass and a brain, we never do."

The map is the basis of all orienteering technique. How the orienteering map is used is as vital as understanding what it is. Getting things right from the start is crucial to all orienteering progression. Grafting other skills onto imperfect map technique is like building a house without foundations.

Orientating the map

The first basic technique is orientating or setting the map, i.e. holding the map in such a way that the direction on the map always corresponds with the direction on the ground. Initially setting the map in this way can be done carefully with direct reference to the terrain detail or by the use of a compass. If you use a compass, which is probably the easiest and most effective method, it can be a simple map guide compass, a thumb compass or a conventional baseplate compass (see appendix B for a description of the various types). The important thing, as with all compass skills, is not what type of compass you use but how you use it.

Fold the map neatly into a comfortable rectangular shape so that the edges accord to the north lines, and hold it in the same hand (left or right) to steer you round the course. As you change direction, change your grip on the map to keep it orientated, and as you steer along your chosen route, along line features or round hills, keep your body behind the map.

Once you understand how to orientate the map, practise it a lot, just as a tennis player or cricketer practices strokes. Other orienteering skills like 'reading ahead' and 'simplifying' can only be developed if the map is orientated correctly the whole time.

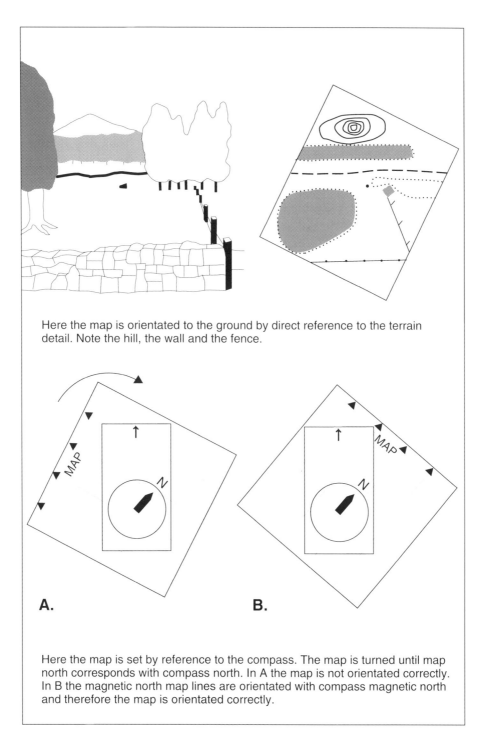

Here the map is orientated to the ground by direct reference to the terrain detail. Note the hill, the wall and the fence.

A.

B.

Here the map is set by reference to the compass. The map is turned until map north corresponds with compass north. In A the map is not orientated correctly. In B the magnetic north map lines are orientated with compass magnetic north and therefore the map is orientated correctly.

Fig 1.7: Orientating the map with reference to the terrain, or with a compass

Practise now just walking or jogging through a forest along a line keeping the map orientated. (Try doing the same with a road map when travelling in a car).

To make this more difficult you can introduce zig-zag sections. Think and read the map ahead, checking features as you proceed to confirm your route. Hold the map so that you can keep your thumb just

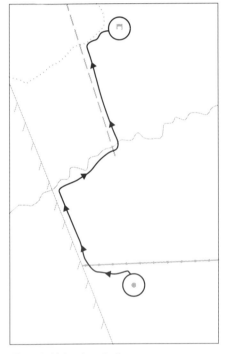

Fig 1.8: Using handrails

beside your position on the map and move it along as you run. Be careful, though, not to obscure detail, so that you can read features both to the left and the right as you follow your line.

If you use a thumb compass, point your direction with the reading tip and sight along the compass arrow. With a conventional protrac-

tor compass, keep checking that the red end of the compass needle accords with the magnetic north lines. Always hold the compass level when you check it.

That's about it then: orientating map to ground is the basic orienteering technique, like a golf swing or weight distribution in skiing. It needs constant practice in training runs and competitions and once it becomes automatic other skills and back-up techniques can be built upon it in an easy logical progression.

Perhaps I could finish by making the other obvious point that reading maps becomes easier the more familiar you are with them. By running with maps, studying them and even surveying and drawing them, you speed up interpretation and visualisation and give added bite to every other orienteering technique. You can even get into the mapper's mind.

Giving the Wood family the best possible start

Let's assume now, that before setting off on the Permanent Course the Woods had had the orienteering map, it's 1:10000 scale and its legend carefully explained to them and had practised reading the orientated map on the tracks beside the Forestry Office. They each have a Silva-type compass and they understand that since the lines on orienteering maps are converted to magnetic north, they can use their compass to orientate the map without any need to correct for variation from true north. With maps orientated in this way they can be

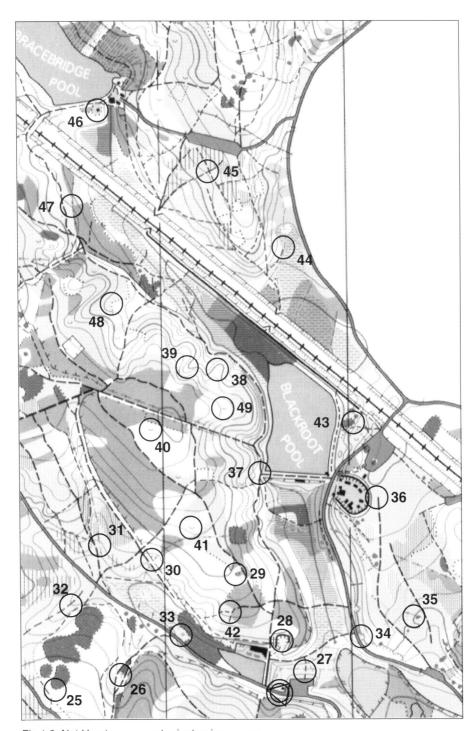

Fig 1.9: Nut Hurst permanent orienteering course

confident that they are going in the right direction and can easily follow the correct paths, tracks and other line features as they proceed.

For a family group of this type, half an hour to an hour is probably enough for an introductory course. Small children need a little less, fit young adults a little more. The first course should link up 6 or so control points which are on or near prominent line features like path junctions, fence corners or stream bends. Following prominent lines on the map like tracks, streams, forest edges or fences is very much like using a road map. Any wrong turnings can be easily corrected by retracing steps, and the control points as they are located give a breathing space and time to set the map ready for the next 'leg'.

Introductory courses which use line features between controls in this way are sometimes called 'handrail' courses, and most of the basic skills build on handrail technique. Ideally, all beginners of all ages and physical condition should tackle several courses of this type before attempting anything more ambitious. The emphasis should not be on finding as many controls as possible but on navigating to all those on the course as quickly as possible. Success is vital in the early stages. The British Orienteering Federation fixture list offers many colour coded events nation-wide and the chart on page 50 illustrates how these relate to the skills ladder. For beginners, white and yellow courses provide the best introduction, though very small children (under 10) can try string courses in which a thread between controls provides a safety handrail - and older fit beginners could try an orange or red course if they are already confident in the basic map skills.

We will see later how the Wood family tackled their first Colour Coded Event, but in the meantime we'll have them practising their new map skills on Sunday walks on the Nut Hurst Permanent Course near their home.

For a brief outline of the philosophy of planning orienteering courses turn to appendix D.

Running with the map orientated

2 The orienteering bug bites again

The Wood family's first flirtation with orienteering might have been its last but for intervention from a most unexpected quarter - Natalie's primary school.

A young teacher had come across orienteering during her college training course, and stumped for ideas on how to make local geography more interesting to 10 year olds on a dull Friday afternoon she decided to get children making their own maps of the classroom and planning mini route-finding courses on them.

"Children - I want you to imagine that this room is a forest, that the tables are groups of trees, and the gangways are paths. Imagine you are sitting in a helicopter above the school and that the roof has been blown off. Now look down and draw a map of our forest. It's a birds' eye view. When you're finished we're going to play a game called orienteering ...."

Natalie suddenly woke up and was soon telling teacher and class about the family orienteering adventure on the permanent course .... "You have a map and find markers in the woods, and sometimes you get lost ...."

Once the spark had taken hold, the lesson taught itself, and Natalie and friends were soon rushing home with the weekend homework to draw maps of their bedrooms.

Success at school tended to dictate Natalie's life pattern and mother

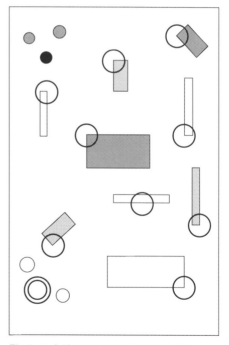

Fig 2.1: A "forest" score exercise in a school gymnasium

and daughter found themselves digging house plans out of the attic, struggling with scales and sharpening pencils .... As Natalie's school lessons in the following weeks took her from classroom and gymnasium into the playground and surrounding fields, inevitably the rest of the family shared her experiences over the evening meal. Natalie's enthusiasm passed on the mysteries of "star games", "handrail courses", "score events" and "mini relays" until at the end of term she

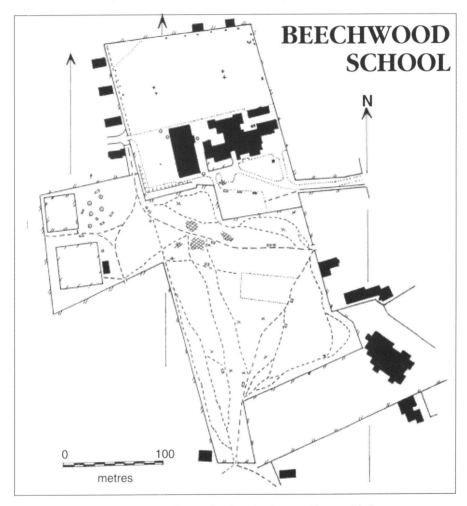

Fig 2.2: Natalie's school map: as later refined and redrawn with expert help

announced proudly that she and two friends were planning a course for the whole class on the new map they had all made (see above).

"We're going to run it like a race and take all the times. Everyone has to punch a special card with a clipper to show they've found every marker ....."

Another spark now took hold, this time in mother's imagination. Helen's calm exterior masked a creative determination which often took the family on

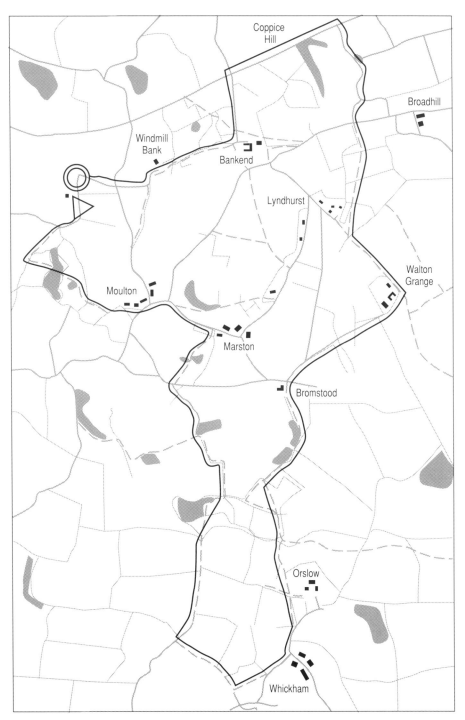

Fig 2.3: A Family Sunday walk, planned like the Wood family course

ventures outside the conventional world of the menfolk. The family Sunday walk that weekend took on a new dimension, as armed with 1:25,000 Ordnance Survey map of their village, mother, father and daughter set off down the bridle path and across the common towed by an eager dog and the prospect of finding the old well which Natalie had chosen as the first checkpoint on the Wood Family Orienteering Course. Each took it in turns to choose the next check point while the other two used the map to navigate to it. From well to bridge to village church - and finally to Coppice Hill, the walk circled its way back to the Wood home and to a welcome Sunday lunch - over which they discussed inadequacies of map and navigational mistakes, while Christopher decided secretly to try the course later with his friend on

Fig 2.4: School orienteering: a pathway to the great outdoors

Fig 2.5: School site orienteering encourages running

their mountain bikes.

In a sense, the family walk had re-enacted the early history of orienteering in Britain where in the early 60's map walks on $2\,^1/2$ inch Ordnance Survey Maps had evolved into recreational orienteering. By the early 1970's, special orienteering maps were being produced from redrawn Ordnance Survey maps, first in black and white at 1:25,000 scale then in several colours at a scale of 1:20,000, and orienteering competitions for all age groups and abilities were being organised on commons, moors and in woods all over the British Isles. Even in these days of photogrammetry and computer drawn maps, many orienteers enjoy doing ground survey and drawing maps for local events - and all competitions are still planned and organised by orienteers themselves.

Natalie's teacher had introduced her children to practical geography through a proven system. Her children learnt map drawing principles, scale and map reading in the familiar environment of the school and then translated their new skills into the wider world of park, wood and common. Map orientation, simple compass work and handrail navigation once learnt and practised, works in the large scale as well as the small scale of classroom and playground, and mother and father learnt the same skills from their daughter on their Sunday excursion. Most of Britain has few wilderness areas but the adaptation of the orienteering philosophy to the public paths, woods and meadows of the countryside is a very attractive model for those - whether on foot, bike or horse - who want to blend exercise, adventure, challenge and aesthetic qualities into a countryside experience.

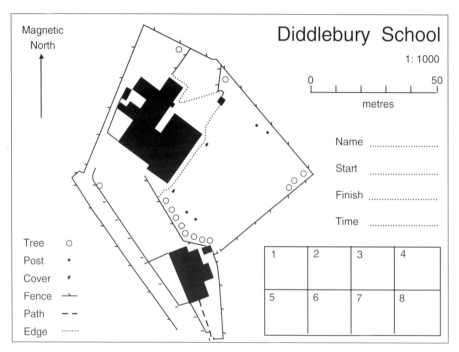

Fig 2.6: A simple school map at a very large scale

Mapping and navigation skills in a school setting

Orienteering is one of the Adventurous Outdoor Activities recommended in the English National Curriculum for Physical Education at key stages 1, 2, 3 and 4, and figures in the Scottish 5-14 Curriculum. It provides obvious cross-curricular links with Geography, Mathematics and Life Style Studies. Detailed advice is to assist the teacher in introducing orienteering in schools available in

Fig 2.7: Courses must be copied accurately from master maps

manuals published in conjunction with the British Orienteering Federation (See appendix H).

Those publications analyse the curriculum and provide a specific series of lesson plans and follow-up activities geared to attainment targets across the curriculum. The skills we touch on here are the core ones, and the extensions and exercises we suggest are central thematic ones capable of many variations.

The foundation skill of map orientation lies at the heart of the school site approach and of all orienteering map reading. Natalie's teacher would have taught the children to fold and orientate their maps and to use them to locate and navigate between marked points in room or playground. She would also

Fig. 2.8: "Which way to the next control?"

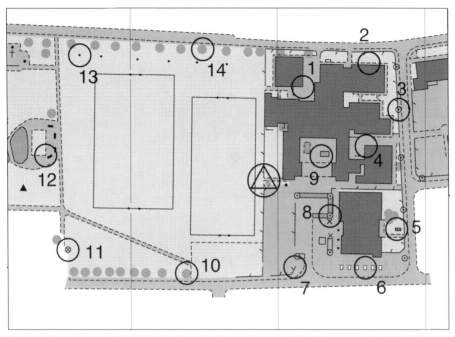

Fig 2.9: School grounds, star exercise: teacher's master with all the controls. Below is the pupil's map, marked with one control.

have shown them how to use their thumbs to mark their position on the map as they progressed round a simple course.

To emphasise these techniques, exercises would be used with frequent changes of direction. The role of the compass would be the simple one of orientating the map and to keeping it orientated with red on the magnetic needle always aligned to magnetic lines on map. The essence of orienteering navigation technique is to keep map and compass together. The compass is used to keep direction accurate while the orienteer reads features from the map. The home-made maps might not be totally accurate but the teacher would ensure that they depicted the correct relationship between objects like tables and

chairs and that lines of buildings and paths were accurate to the extent that they allowed handrail navigation. At this stage the size of map is more important than exact map scale. A4 is easy for a child to handle and scale can be adapted to this.

The teacher would then organise Star Exercises radiating out

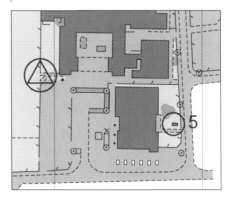

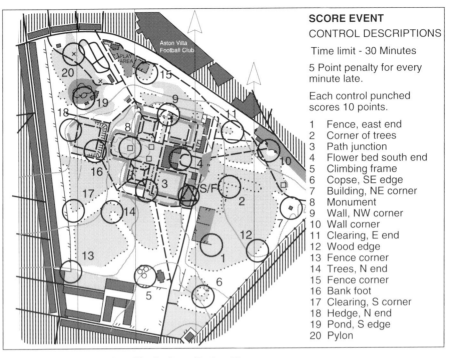

SCORE EVENT

CONTROL DESCRIPTIONS

Time limit - 30 Minutes

5 Point penalty for every minute late.

Each control punched scores 10 points.

1   Fence, east end
2   Corner of trees
3   Path junction
4   Flower bed south end
5   Climbing frame
6   Copse, SE edge
7   Building, NE corner
8   Monument
9   Wall, NW corner
10 Wall corner
11 Clearing, E end
12 Wood edge
13 Fence corner
14 Trees, N end
15 Fence corner
16 Bank foot
17 Clearing, S corner
18 Hedge, N end
19 Pond, S edge
20 Pylon

Fig 2.10: Score event in a Birmingham Park setting

from a central point, score exercises in which pupils would themselves each put out a single marker and then visit as many as possible in a given time, and simple handrail courses, all building upon and extending handrail navigation with an orientated map. Team relays of various types would then be used to introduce an element of team work and problem solving.

The family orienteering walk simply applied the same skills to a larger scale situation, though inevitably rise and fall of the ground introduced some contour appreciation and judgement of ground shapes.

An important element in all this work is the actual production of the map. The basic surveying and drawing of maps, no matter how crude, instils an understanding of the nature of map symbols and the map legend. Children soon learn that all map making involves a certain amount of generalisation. Maps are not an exact representation of the real world but an interpretation of that world as the map maker and navigator see it. Making maps puts the children in the mind of the mapper: it builds up map familiarity and is the most effective way of instilling basic elements of navigation.

It would be nice to think that one of the Wood family would be encouraged to improve on their local Ordnance Survey map and to draw their own map for country walks for themselves and their friends.

3 The first competition: keeping it simple

The two men in the family had found the orienteering footpath course enjoyable but frustrating. Although Chris had covered the ground faster than the family on his mountain bike, he had lost himself several times and at others had made poor route choices which led to unnecessary climbing and detours. Father Michael had wanted to push along faster rather than stopping to study the flowers or admire the views.

Flicking through the local paper one Friday evening, Michael noticed an orienteering results section on the sports page and details of a forthcoming event the following Sunday with the contact phone number of the local club.

"Let's all go along" he suggested. "It's in Badger Woods which is only half-an-hour's drive and we've been there before so we shouldn't find things too difficult."

Samantha had promised her friend Javindar that they would do something different at the weekend so eventually it was 6 who squeezed into the ageing estate car at 9.30 on a misty Sunday morning to set off for the car park field ringed on the Ordnance Survey road map thanks to a grid reference given over the phone.

Making their way diffidently to four cars marked REGISTRATION on the far side of the field, they were confronted with a bewildering choice of courses of various "colours" and distances. Like most club-organised local orienteering events this was a colour-coded event which offered seven courses graded according to length and difficulty. Each was given a colour, from white (the easiest) to brown (most difficult) - see table on page 50.

First they bought one of the colourful maps each: 1:10,000 in scale, covering the total area of the deciduous wood which was about 2km square. Taking advice at registration, they decided to play safe on this first try and to enter easy courses. Natalie, however, didn't take kindly to a suggestion that she try the 'string course' which was set out in a special corner of the wood and linked control markers with a continuous thread, making it virtually impossible to get lost.

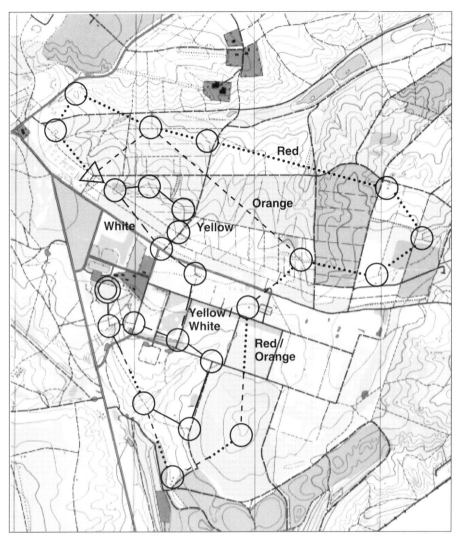

Fig 3.1: The colour coded courses attempted by the Wood family

"That's for little kids" she reacted. "I know how to orienteer from school, so I'll do the 1.5km white course on my own". Samantha and Javindar decided to go round the 2.0km yellow course as a pair, mother Helen opted for the 3.5km orange course and Michael and Christopher for the 5.0km red course, which although still straight forward, had some continuous running between control points, which were spaced further apart than on the short courses. The green (4.5km), blue (6.0km) and brown (8.0km) courses were the territory of experienced orienteers.

Their names were entered on a start list, they were each given a list of control descriptions with marker codes for their course (on each marker there is a code letter or number, see fig 7.2 page 67. They also each received a control card on which was written their name and start time. They were then shown the beginning of the route to the start - a ten minute walk away. This route was indicated by coloured tapes. The Finish banner could be seen on the edge of the assembly field where they were standing, with red and white tapes from it appearing mysteriously from the trees.

They had already been warned that they would have to copy their courses onto their blank maps at the start, so father bought 5 red biros at a convenient stall beside the registration cars - and 5 transparent map cases, just in case it rained or one of them fell in a puddle. They decided to put the

Fig 3.2: Punching must be accurate

control card and description list into the map case for protection, although Christopher pointed out that experienced orienteers seemed to be using a special plastic holder which they pinned to their clothing or looped over a wrist. He also noticed that they copied their control descriptions into the boxes on their control card using a pictograph shorthand.

Fig 3.3: Stretching stiff muscles before the start

The path to the start was already well trodden by a motley file of men, women, girls and boys dressed in what looked like brightly coloured nylon pyjamas. The more fashionable sported lycra tights and fluorescent sweat bands while everyone seemed to be wearing lightweight studded shoes. The Wood family in their ancient tracksuits, jeans and battered trainers felt a bit under-dressed for the occasion.

In the bright forest clearing which served as a start, competitors were stretching stiff muscles, jogging up and down, comparing ailments and injuries, peering at their maps or swapping alibis for the trials to come. A large clock indicated race time, and as their names were called with two minutes to go, the Woods stepped forward, handed in a stub from the control card to register their imminent departure for the forest and waited for the whistle to blow at the 'off' time of 10.45. A quick blast and they were scampering to the master maps with red biros at the ready. Crouched over the course boards, they carefully copied

Fig 3.4: The start, waiting for the "off"

down their courses linking up the numbered red circles carefully with red lines to indicate the correct sequence - and then they were away from the start marker and into the dark forest.

Fortunately, the white and yellow courses shared the same first two controls, and never had Natalie's sisterly feelings been stronger as she followed Samantha down a grassy path straight to the first orange and white marker at a T-junction. A quick glance at the description sheet to check the marker code, a hard squeeze on the plastic needle punch to make a Y shape impression in the first square on the card, and then they were all off to the right along another small path.

34

All Natalie's fears were gone. This was magic. She started to run - so did Samantha and Javindar. The forest grew quieter ... they stopped ... the path stopped. There was no marker, no people. They were lost.

Meanwhile Helen was proceeding at a brisk walk, using the map like a road map, carefully following the lines of paths, field edges, fences and streams until she saw the markers. Other competitors overtook her: some she met two or three times. She wouldn't be hurried. For the first time in her life she was tackling an athletic event and making decisions totally on her own and seeing them justified as she found each control safely. She was completely absorbed in the whole process and as she passed under the Finish Banner and handed in her complete control card some 50 minutes after starting she felt a sense of total satisfaction - before more familiar anxieties about Natalie, Sam and the others took over.

Back in the forest, a tense duel was taking place between a panting Michael, feeling every one of his 42 years and a frustrated Christopher running faster and faster, sometimes in great loops round forest tracks, but always meeting up with his Dad at control points. Michael, wading in a sea of exhaustion, was adopting the reverse tactic of relying more and more on compass bearings which he had learnt years before as a Scout - calculating that straight lines gave his tired brain only one thing to think about and that every metre saved made it more likely that he'd keep going to the Finish. Just over an hour after starting, Chris sprinted past the familiar rolling figure in the Finish straight. Both had

Fig 3.5: Steady but safe on a straight line

made it in their own way. Some 30 minutes earlier Natalie, Sam and Javindar had also finished - albeit after retracing steps back to control one to find the path turn-off they had missed in their haste first time through.

Back in the car, the family changed shoes and socks and compared maps and experiences. Other orienteers of all shapes and ages were studying rows of results stubs hanging from lines along the field fence. Some were discussing their routes, others bewailing mistakes and time lost. The Wood family times figured well down the lists of finishers on their respective courses, though Helen, whose progress had been by far the least frantic, appeared only about half way down on the orange course.

Chris shook his head in stunned disbelief. "Half an hour for 5 kilometres and 45 minutes for 8 kilometres! How do they do it?"

Hopefully in the rest of this chapter, we'll establish how they do it. The Woods' experiences at their first event were fairly typical. All had felt satisfaction at completing the course. None had done anything badly wrong but they had all lost time unnecessarily and over a course of 3-5 kilometres lost seconds and minutes on each leg soon added up. They had been right to choose easy courses, because some degree of success is important for a first experience of any sport, and with orienteering in particular getting badly lost, wet or frightened is hardly likely to encourage a newcomer to have another try.

Apart from Helen on the orange course, the family had failed to keep speed in line with navigational competence and all had ignored the basic skill of keeping in map contact all the time. All beginners should read the map continuously, thumb their progress on it and pay special attention to correct orientation at turning points and on leaving controls. They should plan ahead and try to keep the navigation as simple as possible.

We'll now have a look at the whole area of simplification, hoping that the Woods will gradually absorb and practice the skills described here as they prepare to move up the colour coded scale and perhaps to look forward to more ambitious events in the future - if the orienteering bug continues to bite.

Simplification

Simplification, in bold terms, means simplifying the navigational problems set by the orienteering course planner. The technique involves using the most reliable features on map and ground to reach the control, playing to your own strengths using those skills you can execute best as much as possible, and getting into the mind of the planner. Just as a good batsman at cricket might do some bowling to see problems from another angle, so the good orienteer should understand the principles of course planning so that he or she can foresee 'traps' and develop strategies to solve the problems set by good orienteering courses.

An experienced planner blessed with good orienteering terrain in which to set courses tries to set legs for which the straightest route is the fastest but also requires the most skill in execution. With this in mind the experienced competitor will always be looking for ways in which the navigation can be made easier and/or safer, in other words to simplify the leg so as to get close to the control as quickly as possible and with as little risk as possible.

Simple strategies

Simplification can involve a selection of tactics. For example:

• Line features make useful handrails, as the Wood family quickly discovered. Competitors select and follow linear features that lead towards the control such as paths, streams, field edges, edges of marshes, fences, power lines, earthbanks or ridges. The feature may be followed quickly

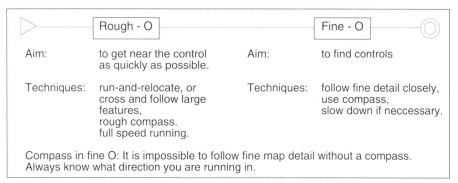

Rough - O		Fine - O	
Aim:	to get near the control as quickly as possible.	Aim:	to find controls
Techniques:	run-and-relocate, or cross and follow large features, rough compass. full speed running.	Techniques:	follow fine detail closely, use compass, slow down if neccessary.

Compass in fine O: It is impossible to follow fine map detail without a compass. Always know what direction you are running in.

Fig 3.6: Rough and fine orienteering

and certainly without the need for further detailed navigation.

• *Splitting legs into easy and hard sections.* Do this so that *Rough-O* technique can cope with the straightforward section and more sophisticated skills are concentrated in the *Fine-O* section which is usually that nearer the control. Use *Rough-O* to run hard to a chosen catching feature (see fig 3.7) or to navigate to an obvious attack point near the control.

• *Aiming off.* If a control is sited on or near a line feature, *aim off* so that when reaching the line feature the way to turn is obvious. Other simplification ideas are:

• *Use of large map features.* Concentrate on *large map features* that are obvious on the ground. It is not necessary to identify each marsh, crag, pit etc. on the illustrated map extract, (fig 3.8) It is enough simply to follow the one large spur. Note that contour features such as this spur, linear ridges, re-entrants and so on can often be used as handrails just like more obvious line features. Similarly, groups of small features like knolls or lines of crags can be treated as one large feature

in providing a simplified mental picture for navigation.

• *Overshoot and come back.* It may be faster and simpler to ignore fine map detail in front of a control if there is a convenient *collecting feature or attack point* just behind the control.

• *Dog leg.* Choose a route to

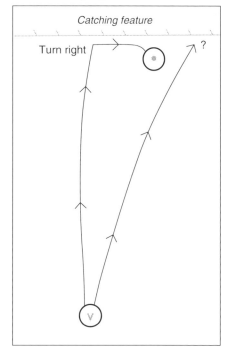

Fig 3.7: Aiming off

the control which allows approach and exit in the same direction - though an experienced planner does not usually leave this option open.

• *Choose a simpler route.* Weigh up obstacles on the direct line to decide whether running round is less physical and less taxing on concentration. For a good runner it may well be faster.

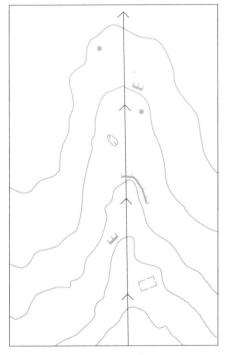

Fig 3.8: Use of large map features

A number of effective training ideas for simplification and handrail orienteering are described in the BOF manual, *The Coaching Collection, Teaching Orienteering* and other books, see appendix H. Some exercises follow.

1. A course can be planned with rough-O sections followed by one or a series of fine-O legs.

Markers can be placed at the 'change of gear' points to bring home the principle of changing speed in accordance with navigational difficulty.

2. Another variation on this theme is the traffic light course with 'green' (fast), 'amber' (slow), and 'red', (walk) sections.

3. Pair training in which orienteers take it in turn to run fast handrail sections and careful fine-O stretches.

4. The type of string line used for small children's courses can be used as an effective handrail to find controls just off the string. This can be particularly useful in coaching children.

Simplification is particularly important in the coaching transition from beginners' courses to courses of intermediate difficulty. It is at this stage that getting round faster becomes more important than merely completing the course without too many problems. On the scale of colour coded courses (see page 50) this marks the transition from Yellow to Orange or Red.

Adjusting speed to the difficulty of the course is, however, an important technique at every competitive level, and with so-called 'continental' terrain in Britain, fast times and consistent performance depend on fast handrail running. The opposite type of terrain is the 'nordic' terrain prevalent in Scandinavia. The same lessons apply but the difficulty for most Britons in their first encounters with orienteering in Scandinavia is in identifying new types of handrail lines. Look particularly for features such as marsh

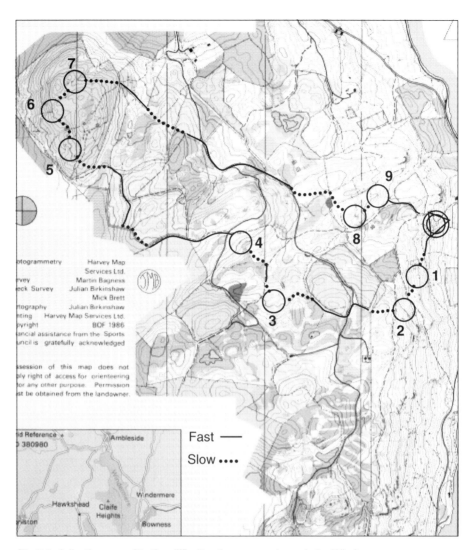

Fast ——
Slow ••••

Fig 3.9: Adjusting speed to the difficulty of a course above Lake Windermere

edges, contour ridges and so on. Once this transition is mastered the principles of simplifying the orienteering can be applied just the same, though maybe at lower speeds.

Now, get out and practise. The next chapter takes the simplification principle one step further with a closer look at the techniques of route choice and the simplification

factors which affect it.

Much of this advice and training work lies in the future for the Wood family but as they quickly discover, closer involvement in the sport soon opens up improvement and training opportunities at club and local level. As their competitive experience broadens we will cover other strategies and training methods

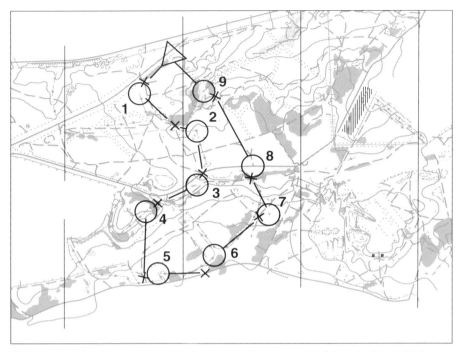

Fig 3.10: Attack point exercise: slow down at the X and use careful navigation to hit the control

which underpin successful orienteering achievement, hoping that like them, you will discover that the better you perform the basic skills, the more satisfaction and pleasure orienteering has to offer.

Your attack point should be easily identifiable

4 Club training: relocation

Before leaving the Badger Woods event Helen had picked up an application form to join the local Darley Orienteering Club and a list detailing future local events. There was no dissent when she suggested taking out a joint family membership for which one fee included membership of club, region and British Orienteering Federation. Although each member of the family now had different expectations from orienteering, all decided they wanted to have another go - and this time to do better.

A few days later, a club magazine and fixture list plopped through the letter box and the Woods were faced with the decision on how far to take their new commitment. Both parents wanted to try one of the Tuesday evening training sessions. Chris, Samantha and Natalie were less sure. None of their friends were orienteers and as the club met in the Youth Centre of a local rival school, teenager politics entered the equation. Eventually, parent pressure won over Chris and Natalie. Samantha insisted that Tuesday was a busy homework evening and chose to miss out first time round. She decided to wait and see what the others felt before making up her mind for the future.

Luckily Darley Orienteering Club was an active organisation which treated orienteering in the widest of perspectives. Tuesday evening training took place winter and summer and involved a wide mix of physical and technical training, as well as social activities like quizzes, parties, orienteering bingo, car rallies and fund raising. Club coaches gave follow-up sessions after Sunday competitions and advised on event entries and preparation for important occasions like Championships. Winter evenings centred on gym and road runs, summer on technical training and activities in local woods. The club membership was about 100 and covered all ages and abilities. Many families were involved in mapping, organising and helping with transport to events as well as in competing most weeks of the year. Summer camping weekends combined with competitions in scenic parts of the countryside were particular family favourites.

The Woods approached the Youth Centre at 7.00pm with some trepidation. They did not consider themselves athletes and they were unsure what exactly was to be organised and how it related to orienteering. They found a variety of activities on offer - circuit training in the gymnasium, a choice of 'pack runs' round the local estate on a complicated street map, a map discussion/ post mortem on the Badger Woods event, and later that evening a team shuttle map relay in the Gymnasium.

This last activity involved transferring a course from a master map at one end of the room to a blank map at the other. Each member of a team took one control circle at a time and the first team to accurately transfer the complete course was adjudged the winner. Natalie and her mother very much enjoyed this, particularly as Chris' boys' team, having completed the exercise very quickly was disqualified for a wrongly placed control circle. They were pleased to hear that variations on the map relay theme were a regular Tuesday evening favourite. Michael found a discussion over routes taken

Fig 4.1: Explaining the Team Shuttle Relay

on the previous Sunday very valuable in establishing how he had lost time and was relieved to find that even the experts made mistakes. The better orienteers seemed to re-find themselves extremely quickly, however, and Michael made a mental note to discover what methods they used to relocate themselves so quickly. They also learnt how to put control card and description list into one hand-held unit to save time in punching at controls. Chris found himself initiated into the mysteries of international control descriptions which, as he had spotted at Sundays' event, were used as a shorthand for transferring descriptions onto control cards as well as overcoming language problems at major events where several nationalities might be taking part (see appendix C).

Much against his better judgement, Chris tried the circuit round a series of repetition exercises on benches, wall bars and ropes in the gym. It was tough, but much to his surprise he kept going much better than many others, and buoyed up with confidence decided to do a 2 kilometre street run afterwards.

Come 9.00pm and time to go, both parents and children had found new friends and were already noting down venue and details for the next competition in a fortnight's time. There was no question now that the Woods were hooked on orienteering but Helen couldn't help wondering whether all this involvement and exercise was going to make them any better at it. This question will be answered in the pages which follow.

Orienteering involves thinking and decision making as well as running. Facility with maps builds up map reading experience and confidence. Analysis of performances helps in diagnosing weaknesses and developing training strategies to eradicate them. Physical fitness provides a basic conditioning which can take some of the pain out of competitions, reduce the pressure of map reading while in extreme fatigue or oxygen debt, and provide a foundation for those motivated to pursuing more ambitious goals. Running over uneven ground or ducking under trees also demands flexibility and so exercises to develop suppleness were also built into the gym circuits. The summer training programme included exercises to improve a sequence of orienteering skills. More formal coaching was provided at a once a month 'clinic' held on Saturday mornings.

The Woods now had a foot on the first rung of the orienteering ladder, but already family ideas and ambitions were diverging. Helen had decided that greater fitness would speed her up round the next course with the additional spin-off of reducing an expanding waistline. Michael could see that improved map reading and attention to relocation and route choice strategies could compensate for lack of speed and fitness. Chris had his eyes on joining two other lads in a club relay team for the Regional Championships while Natalie had heard from her new friends of a summer training camp in the Lake District. Samantha didn't need much persuading later that evening that she should join the training circus on the following Tuesday.

We will return to physical training for orienteering in much more detail in chapters 9 and 10 where there are indoor and outdoor training ideas. An example of an event analysis sheet which can be used to follow up competition performance is to be found in chapter 8, page 81. Here we will isolate Michael's concern about relocation and examine this whole concept in detail. Relocation can be vital in reducing time lost from hours to seconds. Some skills dealt with here lie far beyond the Woods' experience, particularly in the field of ground shape visualisation, but the relocation concept makes more sense when looked at as a whole.

Relocation

Whatever our level of orienteering experience or skill there will come a time (often sooner rather than later) when we become lost. Knowing what to do in such a situation is therefore essential.

Relocation is a valuable orienteering skill but its relative importance in the wider scale of orienteering technique remains, for some, a matter of debate. Some people would argue that good coaching practice should accentuate the positive and that, especially with beginners, it is more important to instil confidence by emphasising positive achievement than to dwell on what might go wrong. Nursery stories have a lot to answer for in encouraging attitudes which result in children (and a few adults) being afraid to venture into the big, bad wood for fear of wolves, bears and other unfriendly creatures.

My own feeling is that teachers and coaches should introduce relocation skills fairly early on in the climb up the technique staircase.

It is important, however, to make sure that relocation is given a positive emphasis. Some coaches even talk about 'continuous relocation' in the sense that when an orienteer combines simplification with fast running on a compass bearing, the exact location at any given moment on a leg is generally not known. The runner must therefore be constantly looking to com-

Fig 4.2: Where am I?

pare map to ground for evidence with which to establish current position as accurately as possible.

Too much contact with the map slows down progress; too little and continuous relocation quickly becomes static relocation, which can lose seconds or minutes depending upon your relocation system and your skill in applying it.

Relocation on the run

Here an experienced orienteer may be running hard on compass with a simplified image of the leg in mind. Pace counting will be used as a back-up in order to calculate the distance travelled. Catching features will confirm the route and if either distance check or compass start ringing alarm bells, should slow down, divert to an adjacent handrail or look for an obvious ground feature which will confirm position and thereby restore confidence.

Every piece of map and terrain is unique to itself; even a blank featureless area tells you something. In general, on the coarse section of a leg continuous relocation means that, like a low flying pilot, you keep going whilst always keeping constantly alert for map or ground features which will help to confirm your position.

Relocation near the control

Once you are near to the control a different relocation technique is required. If things don't fit within the circle the first thing you must do is orientate your map with the compass (see fig 1.7, page 19). Next, look at map and ground for clear features to establish your precise position. This usually works and you can then read yourself into the control. If it doesn't work, or the control isn't where you expected it to be, then you must face up to the fact that you are lost!

Relocation when lost

No matter how experienced you are, the first rule when you are lost is not

RELOCATION

1. When alarm bells ring, **STOP**, **LOOK** and **LISTEN**.
Don't look for, or follow, other people.

2. Try to remember where you were on the map the last time
you were certain of your position.

3. Orientate the map. **CONCENTRATE HARD**.

4. How far have you come, and what have you passed?

5. Look around you, try to find a large or clear feature to identify, on
the ground and on the map.

6. Note its relationship to other smaller features.

7. If you are in a featureless area this may be significant.
Negative orienteering.

8. Have you made a parallel error?

9. What other mistake could you have made?

10. You are still lost!

11. Take a compass bearing to a large line feature this time, for example
to a field edge or road, noting your direction of travel and remember
ing any terrain details.

12. If you are still lost and unhappy retrace your steps to the last point at
which you can be certain of your position, even if this means the
previous control or start, if you are lost looking for control 1.

Fig 4.3: Steps to take when relocating

to waste time by wandering around looking for the marker or other orienteers. Admit that you are lost and start taking positive steps to relocate yourself. Stop running and examine your map carefully. Compare your map 'picture' with the terrain about you.

If this fails to help, then look for the last point on the map where you were certain of your position. Next, project your route forwards and see if you can spot the feature or features that you can identify about you. If this works, and everything fits, then you are in business, but remember to start off carefully; you are at your most vulnerable after a mistake.

If you still cannot locate your position then you must either go back to your last known point or, if this is some distance back and there are clear features not too far off your route (e.g. a field corner or path junction), make for this known feature and, having identified it, proceed from there.

The basic guidelines to be applied in relocating are: (a) make for a known point, (b) don't keep running in the hope that you may stumble across the control or some other orienteer, and (c) take it slowly and calmly.

Panic shuttling backwards and forwards or going round in ever decreasing circles inevitably gener-ates mistakes later on in the course even if by doing so you are lucky enough to find the control. Above all, once you have relocated, avoid the temptation to run off fast in an attempt to make up time. Ease yourself back into the race carefully.

It is worth stressing at this point that skill in relocation often seems to mark the distinction between the good and the not-so-good orienteer. In looking at the routes of young elite Scandinavian orienteers, I've often been surprised by the fact that, on average, they make just as many mistakes as their British counterparts. The difference lies in their ability to minimise the time lost due to these mistakes. British juniors often lose minutes on one error due to poor relocation technique whereas young Swedes measure their mistakes in seconds.

From a very early age, young Scandinavians train and compete in complicated, heavily contoured forests. Inevitably they build up accurate terrain visualisation and map memory skills which then make relocation much easier and more consistent. It is no accident that the 'run and relocate' technique of orienteering was developed in the ridge, knoll and marsh areas of

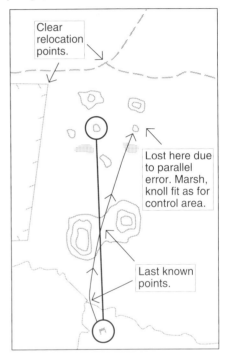

Fig 4.4: Normal relocation procedure

Scandinavia where speed depends upon simplification and fast running into the control circle.

On one occasion I recall a young British orienteer took this technique to its extreme. On a leg which ended with a control in a very complex area, he chose to ignore the difficult contour detail leading up to the control, electing instead to

46

deliberately overshoot to a road junction beyond the control, returning to the flag cleanly and with a very fast time for the leg.

Look at the example in figure 4.4. What is the best relocation strategy? Back to the saddle (see fig 7.1 for some contour terms) or stream junction or forward to the path junction? Ultimately, the decision will probably rest on your fitness and level of performance but whatever you decide you will always be more successful if you employ a logical relocation strategy based on a calm and rational decision than if you panic and trust to hope, luck or the shirt-tails of a passing orienteer.

Figures 4.5 and 4.6 describe two very effective ways of training relocation skills, both of which are used extensively in Sweden to instil in juniors an appreciation of map visualisation and re-contact drills. Both rely on pairs of orienteers sharing a map which is then passed from one to another to force relocation either in mid-leg or near the control circle. The map with the control shown is handed over within the large circle, so that the orienteer has to locate the exact position and find the control. One orienteer runs with the map, one without. For continous relocation, both have maps but only one has the control shown.

'Follow John' exercises of this type also give valuable feedback, not only on your partner's technique but also on your own. They improve map-to-ground and ground-to-map skills and also improve concentration.

This exercise can also be done with a group passing the map around, or a series of maps with different control points being handed out 200 metres or so from the end of a leg.

Martin Bagness, the former British champion, recommends a similar exercise for mid-leg relocation. The map is transferred between runners mid-leg as a training strategy for the run-and-continuous-

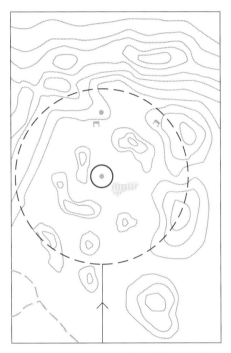

Fig 4.5: Training relocation skills near the control

relocation technique. This also trains the ability to run on a compass bearing even when contact is temporarily lost, confident that relocation is imminent.

Hanging control markers for training exercises also builds up terrain and map visualisation and trains relocation skills.

In all these exercises, the

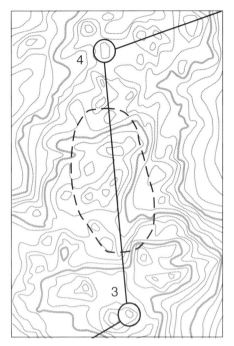

Fig 4.6: Mid leg relocation. The map is
exchanged in the dotted area.

orienteers must work together not
against each other. This is an
important principle in all orienteering
training and coaching. The best
orienteers learn more from each
other than all the coaches and
training manuals in the world.

Relocation: Head for a major feature

5 Moving up the ladder: route choice

In the months after joining the club, the Wood family's orienteering education progressed vigorously if not always smoothly. A succession of Colour Coded events (see table on page 50) saw Natalie moving quickly from white to yellow and using her natural running speed to spearhead the results lists regularly. Helen and her husband both moved up to light green where "*slow but sure*" versus "*hit or miss*" approaches led to lively Sunday evening discussions on the best route choices and mutual mistakes. Both had already learnt that most mistakes were due to lack of concentration rather than incompetence and that a sure-fire situation to generate a mistake was to meet each other or a friend on the course. The whole family now enjoyed marking in their routes on their maps on Sunday evenings, adding up time lost through mistakes and comparing notes with each other and friends.

Chris had skipped light green for the more difficult green courses but although his weekly training had given him the necessary fitness and speed for a good result he constantly got 90% of the course right but lost ten minutes or more on just one or two legs - usually through running too fast at the beginning or end of courses.

Samantha had settled for orange with the goal of getting round at under 10 minutes per kilometre and thereby getting in to the top 25% on the course. Three performances in the top 50% had already won her an orange badge, but as a perfectionist she was still determined to get it absolutely right and reach the Mecca of every orienteer, a perfect run.

Once a month during the winter and spring the Darley Dale Club held a training session for those wishing to correct weaknesses and improve technique. The Woods had entered a Spring Badge Event in their respective age classes and decided that a tune-up beforehand would be no bad thing. All except Natalie, who had a school music rehearsal on Saturday mornings, turned up and joined 25 others in the Forest Car Park to hear one of the club coaches explain the morning's exercise, which was designed to improve route choice and decision making under competition pressure.

Colour	Length km	Technical level	Control sites	Type of leg	Time mins	Age	Step
String	0.8	Very easy	On the line		10	3+	1
White	1-1.5	Easy	Major line features and junctions	Line features: minimal route choice	20	6-12	1
Yellow	1-2.5	Easy	Line features and very easy adjacent features	Line features: easy route choice; no compass	30	8+	2
Orange	2-3.5	Medium	Minor line and easy point features	Route choice - collecting features near control	45	10+	3
Red	4-5.6	Medium			50		4
Green	4-5.6	Hard	Small point and contour features	Fine compass and contours; more physical	50		4
Blue	4.5-6.5	Hard			60		4+
Brown	6.5+	Hard			75		4+

Fig 5.1: Colour coded courses in the BOF Competition Structure

The group was divided into roughly matched pairs and each was given a map on which the course circles were linked by a red line and a blue line - indicating two different routes which roughly balanced out in terms of distance and difficulty. Runners had to try and beat their partners to the first control, one following the red and the other the blue line. After a quick rest and exchange of notes, the process would be repeated for the rest of the 6 controls which completed the course. After that the fit ones could go round again having swapped colour with their partners. This way, some would be covering 4km, others 8km. For the fast, fit and accurate, the session developed into hard interval training (see chapter 10 page 107) along the paths and tracks, with a recovery stop at each control; for others it was more a case of tortoise versus hare and simply getting it right.

By the time the family piled back in the car to dash back home for a late lunch they all felt as tired as after a normal orienteering competition, though in the excitement of beating one another to the markers, fatigue had been masked by the cloak of concentration.

"I've just measured how far I ran", Samantha commented as she studied the map afterwards. "It said 4km in straight lines but I ran 5km. I could never have done that round the school field."

Chris found he had covered 9km - "That's nearly 6 miles - and most of it fast - and I didn't make any mistakes. I must be getting better."

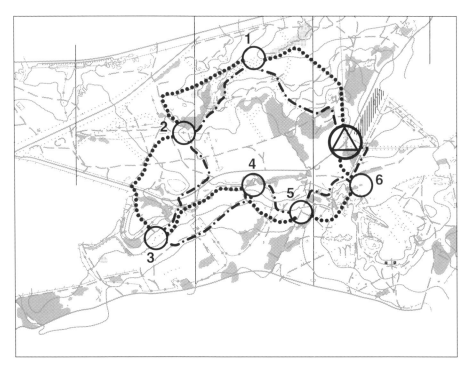

Fig 5.2: Family route choice training exercise

Helen and Michael were more guarded. They had already learnt that in orienteering pride often comes before a fall and that anything approaching their route choice exercise speed in the following Sunday's Badge Event would surely bring swift retribution. Moreover, the route choices on the training exercise had required little more than the basic skill of handrail orienteering. Badge Event Courses would demand simplification, compass and perhaps contour skills too.

In the meantime, let's take a closer look at the concept of route choice and its application to orienteering. The Woods were tackling it in a very crude form at this stage, but in many ways route choice is the essence of orienteering. In the section which follows we make no excuses for making a detailed examination of route choice all its forms and at all levels - albeit we touch on skills beyond the Wood family experience so far.

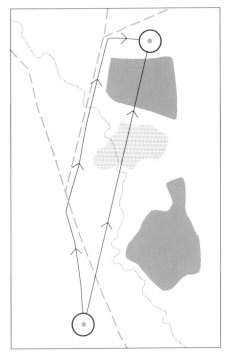

Fig 5.3: Through or round?

Route choice

Route choice is not just a matter of using the information on the map; you must also know your own strengths and weaknesses, and apply this knowledge before reaching your decision. What is also required is both *choosing the best route* and then *executing* it successfully. The problem lies in what is best. The straight line may be the fastest, but if the planner is doing the job properly this will also be the most difficult route to execute.

In weighing up the simplification strategies discussed in chapter 3, the average orienteer may well decide to follow a pattern of paths which involves extra distance, but is a safer route for the level of expertise attained so far. The unfit competitor may choose a gentler, *round* route in preference to the *straight line* over a hill or through a marshy area. The good technical orienteer will always be looking for *short cuts* both in technical and physical terms. So let's look now at some basic principles which govern route choice.

The first and rather surprising guideline is that in estimating a leg, the end is more important than the beginning. It's vital to look at the best line into a control and then to plan a route back from that. Very often this means locating a clear attack point: it's even better if there are obvious checkpoints as the control gets nearer. The chances are that mental and physical powers will be lower towards the end of a leg than at the beginning, so if there are to be tricky physical or technical

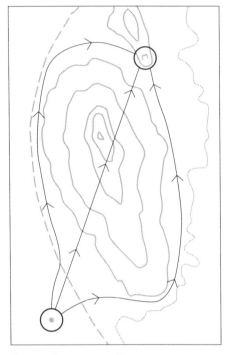

Fig 5.4: Over or round?

sections it's better to tackle them earlier rather than later in the leg.

This argument also applies to the whole orienteering course. Competitors having a good run should concentrate on safe route choices towards the end of a course when the temptation is to take more risks. Elite races are often won and lost in the last ten per cent of the course, and planners are fond of putting in short tricky legs as the finish gets closer. A favourite device is to plan legs diagonally across steep hill sides so that any overshoot

involves a harsh physical penalty.

Another rule of thumb is to be extra careful after making a mistake. Never take a risky route choice to try and catch up lost time. That way, a two minute mistake can become five minutes.

Remember that success in orienteering depends as much as anything on maintaining concentration during long periods of physical and mental stress. If you can give yourself a physical and psychological rest by taking a slightly longer forest road run at some point on a course, this may bring dividends

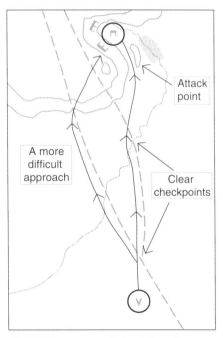

Fig 5.5 Plan your route back from the next control

later. Some elite performers will use such a rest to plan route choices for the rest of the course, though this can be a dangerous strategy for beginners. For the average competitor the best tactic is to concentrate

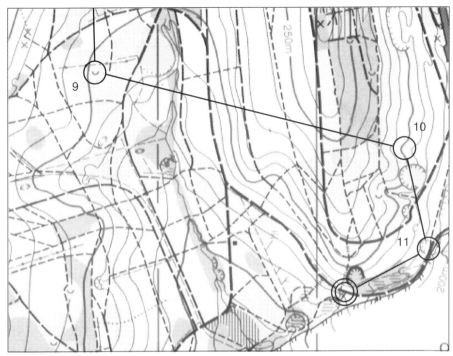

Fig 5.6: A diagonal hill leg

hard on one leg at a time. As one orienteer explained to me: "I see each control as the end of the world."

Having said this, its a good idea to have a plan for the next leg as you approach each control. This allows a smooth run in and out in the right direction which, with quick, sure punching, develops the smooth control flow that saves those precious seconds, which can add up surprisingly as the course unfolds.

Unfortunately, there is sometimes a tendency for British planners to produce courses which are control-picking exercises rather than navigational races through turning points provided by controls. This means that on a course there may be just one or two route choice legs which need sorting out in the terms I

have discussed. In Scandinavia it is quite common to have route choice legs for most of the course. Complicated terrain can make a hard mental, as well as physical, exercise. A 7km course may well have only 8 or 9 legs but each requires intense concentration and skill to stay on course. On an elite course the final race result may hinge on making correct route choices on one or two long legs. In a recent Swedish 5 Days race, the choice on leg 4 lay between 2km straight or 3^1/2km round a track system. Post race analysis showed the run round to be faster. It also was easier to 'read' and allowed forward planning for the rest of the course.

Finally, it is worth stressing that whatever the route choice, on most occasions in conventional orienteering (as opposed to mountain orienteering) there will be a relatively small time difference between the various alternatives. The vital factor is execution. So in balancing up 100 metres of extra running as against 30 metres of climb or 100 metres of 'fight' as against 300 metres of 'fast run', remember that it is your abilities which will dictate the success or otherwise of the route choice decision. So, if you're fast over the ground but weak technically, run round difficult areas. The main thing is to get it right.

The route choice exercise tackled by the Wood family had been a good one. Pairs (or threes) running different routes against each other for each leg, with a rest at the control to compare notes, can produce a terrain interval session of physical training as well as excellent technical feedback. Score events (see appendix A) can also sharpen up route decision making. Don't forget too that a sports watch makes it possible to compare leg times over a whole training course or event course.

As I have said before, the most successful training strategies involve learning from and helping others, and in no other technical area can this be more valuable than in route choice. In Scandinavia as in Britain, coaches are thin on the ground relative to numbers of competitors and the very nature of orienteering makes it difficult to get accurate feedback on forest performance. Few orienteers in Britain have the luxury of a fast coach to

Name of Orienteer   **Name of Shadower**

Leg	Looks at map	Uses compass	Route choice	Execution
S to 1				
1 to 2				
2 to 3				
3 to 4				
4 to 5				
5 to 6				
6 to 7				
7 to 8				
8 to F				
Total				
General comments				

Fig. 5.7: Recording sheet used by a coach or friend to monitor performance round a course

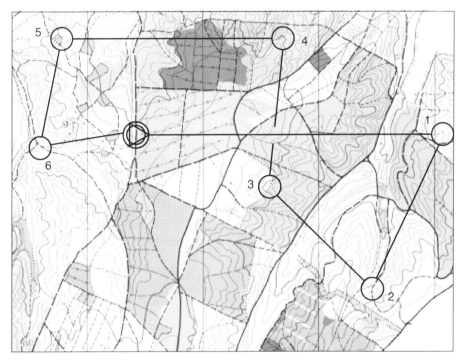

Fig. 5.8: 5km route choice course

shadow them, but most have friends of similar ability and there are frequent events the year round to use for training. So all that has to be done is to get out there and practise.

In the meantime, take a look at some of the route choices pre-sented in figure 5.8 and see which routes you would take. Remember, plan back from the control, look for attack points, checkpoints, physical and technical difficulties, and assess them in the light of your own ability.

Route choice: Consider even the least likely routes, as long as there is a safe attack point for the control

6 The badge event and compass skills

The Sunday Badge Event (see page 131 for an explanation of the Badge Scheme) was on suburban heath land about half an hour's drive from the Wood's home. Because the terrain was so flat and interlaced with paths, the course lengths were longer than the family was used to, and the map at 1:15,000 was at a smaller scale than they had used before. Entry in advance had brought control cards with start times and race details through the letter box about a week beforehand, so they all knew they were off at 11.18 on their respective courses and that there was a 15 minute taped walk to the start.

Natalie's W11A course was 2.7km, Samantha's W13A was 4.0km, Chris M15A 7.0km, Helen's W40S 4.5km and Michael's M45S 5.5km. The junior classes proceeded in 2 year age bands; the older classes in 5 year bands. The age number indicated the first year in the class for the current year from 1st January. Sam's class therefore included girls (W) aged 13 in the current year and also those in the year above (i.e. 14), Michael's included men (M) 45 and 4 years above (i.e. up to 49). The Junior classes (up to and including M19) had A and B classes, the Senior Classes Long and Short. B classes were both physically and technically easier than the A classes. Short courses tended to be of the same technical level but much easier physically. Typically, the parents had played safe in choosing their classes. The children reacted against the B label and went for broke, though Chris in particular was surprised by the length of his course - and the 17 controls he had to visit.

Because of the fast, flat terrain, the planner had tried to cut out too much path running for the more difficult courses by setting most legs across the path systems to small features like pits and knolls between them. This meant that, apart from Natalie's course which mostly followed paths, all the courses had more control points than normal.

The family viewed their competition prospects with mixed feelings. While they welcomed the lack of contour detail and steep slopes for which their experience had still not prepared them fully, the less detailed nature of the area and small control sites meant that navigation had to be very accurate with precise use of compass vital. It was no surprise therefore that Michael, who had concentrated on compass technique from his first ventures into orienteering should have achieved the best result, though even he found himself overshooting obscure small gullies and pits and having to take back bearings from path junctions to find the controls. Since his boyhood as a Scout, he had always enjoyed taking compass bearings (see page 61) and tackling forest games and treasure hunts in straight lines. Here on Ashridge Heath he was in his element. Helen and Samantha were less certain and after early disasters lost in a sea of path junctions both settled for safe routes round paths rather than across. Chris followed a path running strategy from the start and although he ran nearer 9km than 7km in completing his course, he was pleased to see himself up in the first 20 in the results. Natalie, as usual had flown round her course in 25 minutes and to her delight finished 3rd, only 30 seconds behind the winner.

Since this was a National Badge Event, performances could count towards a Gold (within 25% of the average of first 3 times), Silver (within 50%) or Bronze (within 100%) Badge in the National Badge award system. Three results were needed to achieve the appropriate standard.

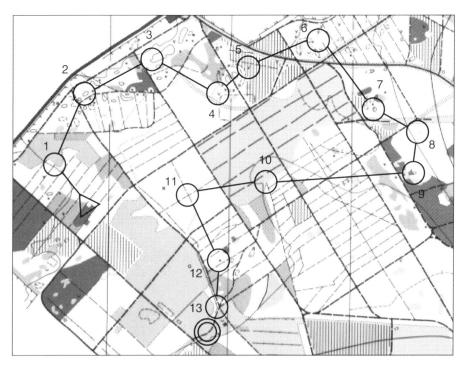

Fig 6.1: Samantha's map: which controls do you think she found difficult?

All agreed afterwards that Michael's compass navigation strategy was theoretically the best if done accurately and adjusted to the right speed for each leg. However, slowing down for difficult controls on point features (e.g. a

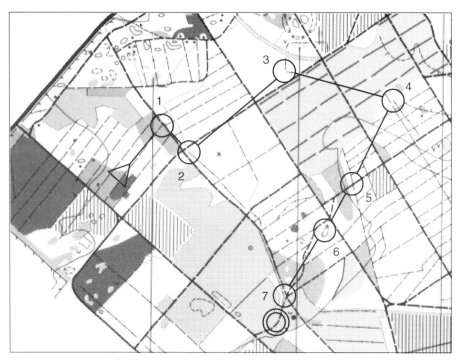

Fig 6.2: Natalie's map: on which legs could distance judgement have helped?

boulder) needed a lot of self discipline when the ground was such fast beech forest and even on the easy stretches it was important to count paths and keep contact with the map. Even Natalie had overshot some controls and felt it would have been useful to have been able to judge how far she had run along a path when it came to turning into the trees to find the control.

The routes which they drew in on their maps afterwards all included a lot of mazy squiggles near the control circles and diversions out to prominent path junctions and clearings to relocate after mistakes. They all agreed that compass and distance training were aspects of their orienteering they now needed to concentrate upon and decided to suggest this to the Club Training Committee as an exercise worth putting into the summer training programme.

Let's look at the whole area of compass work now and see how it fits into orienteering strategies. Whether using the compass simply as an orientation instrument with the map, or using it to take bearings, it is obviously a vital direction-finding tool, and if the direction is right, map reading along that line becomes much easier, as the Woods had quickly discovered. Whilst map reading remains the fundamental orienteering skill, compass and distance judgement skills are the basic back-up. We will look at them together but first we will examine in detail the process of taking a compass bearing.

Compass and pacing

We're going to look at compass work in the two key areas of *rough* and *fine* orienteering and see how, when combined with distance judgement, an orienteering strategy can be developed which is often summed up as *Compass and Pacing*.

I will not be advocating one

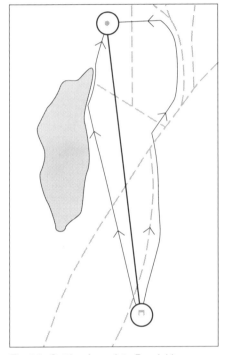

Fig 6.3: Getting from A to B quickly

type of compass in preference to another (see Appendix B for a description of types of compasses). Elite orienteers use both thumb and conventional protractor compasses (although from my own experience I think that it is fair to say that the precision use of a thumb compass needs a closer application to its operation than most British orienteers accord it.) My aim, as

always, is to define and then apply basic techniques.

Let's look at a common situation in which skilful use of the compass can get you from A to B quickly. Figure 6.3 shows a typical leg in a flattish British forest with plenty of line features.

Many competitors would follow the path system since, at first glance, it appears the safest. But executing this route choice requires care in hitting the right paths. I suggest that the quickest strategy (and maybe even the safest) is to run fast on a compass bearing to the lake end and then to use slow and accurate compass technique to locate the boulder. It would be wise to aim off a little to the left to avoid missing the lake but in reality it is unlikely that you would fail to see it, however thick the forest.

These two differing compass techniques are often referred to as *rough* compass (running to the lake) and *fine* compass (navigating to the boulder). In truth I do not like the term rough compass. Whenever a compass is used the emphasis should be on accuracy. This means getting the body behind the compass, letting the needle settle and using sighting points in the forest to keep on a precise line. How often have I seen juniors (and seniors) zigzagging through rough forest with thumb compass and map thumping up and down in their hand like a relay baton.

These two complementary compass techniques can be developed and refined for all types of flat to moderate terrain. Even in detailed Swedish forests elite competitors

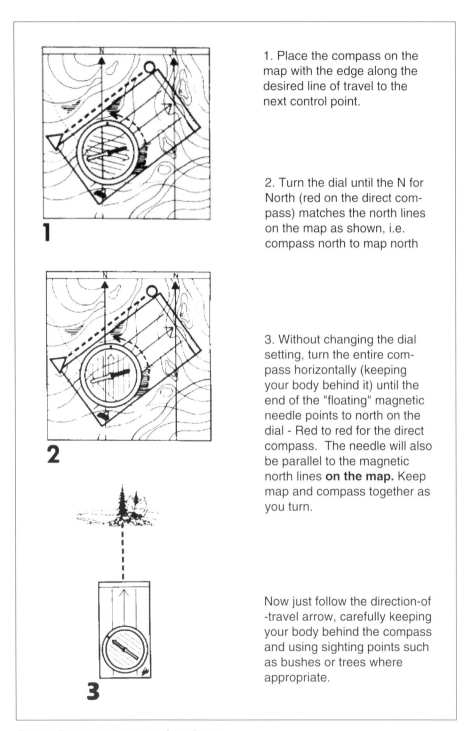

1. Place the compass on the map with the edge along the desired line of travel to the next control point.

2. Turn the dial until the N for North (red on the direct compass) matches the north lines on the map as shown, i.e. compass north to map north

3. Without changing the dial setting, turn the entire compass horizontally (keeping your body behind it) until the end of the "floating" magnetic needle points to north on the dial - Red to red for the direct compass. The needle will also be parallel to the magnetic north lines **on the map.** Keep map and compass together as you turn.

Now just follow the direction-of-travel arrow, carefully keeping your body behind the compass and using sighting points such as bushes or trees where appropriate.

Fig 6.4: Taking a bearing: the Silva System

can simplify navigational problems by the application of a 'run fast and relocate' technique which depends on the accurate use of compass coupled with distance judgement and close observation of terrain

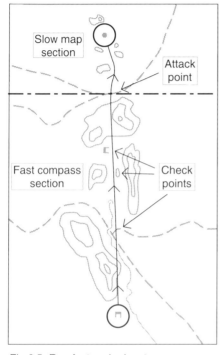

Fig 6.5: Run fast and relocate

final verdict on technique.

So how does distance judgement fit into all this? Essentially it is another back-up tool. If you know how far you have travelled as well as the direction you have taken, location should be relatively easy. The most effective method of judging distance is to know how many paces you take for a given 100 metres. It is easier to count double paces (i.e. every time either your left or right foot strikes the ground) but you will have to make allowances for gradients (up and down) and terrain (forest, moorland, parkland). This

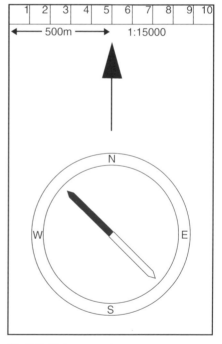

Fig 6.6: Distance scale on a compass

detail once near the control. In theory, since reading off a lot of fine detail slows the competitor down, eliminating the need to read the map over the greater part of the leg by using the compass allied to ground-to-map observation to check progress can save a lot of time.

It should be stressed that this is a risky strategy. It requires self discipline, concentration, sound compass technique and an ability to control one's running speed. Nevertheless, it can produce fast times and in the end the result gives the

means remembering a number of different pace counts or applying some weighting to your basic count and it is these variables which ultimately makes pace counting such a hit and miss affair. Nevertheless, it is better than no system at all.

Once you have established your pace count you can keep this information readily available by making a pace scale for 1:15,000 or 1:10,000 as appropriate and sticking

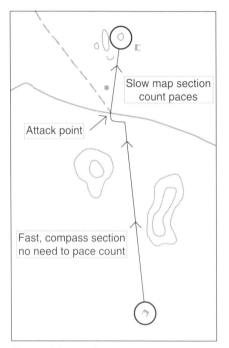

Slow map section count paces

Attack point

Fast, compass section no need to pace count

Fig 6.7: It is not always necessary to pace count

it to the leading edge of your compass. I prefer to think distance rather than paces and for this reason I like to use the distance scales with 100 metre splits which are a feature of some orienteering compasses.

Elite orienteers will often boast that they don't count their paces. In truth they probably did once upon a time but now, with several years of experience behind them, they have become able to judge distance subconsciously.

Perhaps I could quote my old friend Borje Palmkvist again. When he was talking to a junior squad group at Ludvika in Sweden he said, "I read the map carefully and check features as I pass them. I run on a bearing and adjust my compass as I pass my checkpoints. I count paces all the time, starting again after each checkpoint. This way I always find the controls!"

On one occasion Borje's marked up route after an event showed an attack point on a blank piece of the map. When questioned about this by one of the juniors he replied, "I paced on an exact bearing for 100 metres. When I stopped I said to myself: this is my attack point. From there I found the control easily." Borje's technique is probably too slow these days for elite success but he rarely loses an H50 race and is incredibly consistent. It is not difficult to see why. (In international competition male and female classes are designated by an H and D respectively, from the German Herren, men and Damen, women).

One last point before I finish. Although I would argue that the compass should be used as a back-up to map reading at every event, every time (because it never lies), it isn't always necessary to pace count. If a leg crosses a forest road or another type of obvious line feature then there is no point in religiously counting your paces up to it - unless, of course, you're doing it for practice!

You'll find in figs. 6.8-6.11 (overleaf) ideas for compass and distance training. Practice makes perfect, and the use of the compass should become automatic - like ski poles to a skier. It's not a bad idea, therefore, to get used to carrying a compass on training runs and running diagonals across familiar blocks of forest, or even pace counting between lamp posts on road runs.

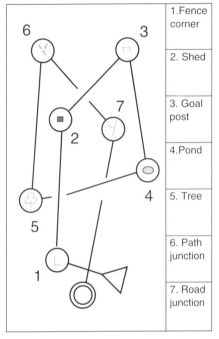

1.Fence corner	
2. Shed	
3. Goal post	
4.Pond	
5. Tree	
6. Path junction	
7. Road junction	

Fig 6.8: Compass and distance training course, without a map.

1. A rough orienteering course can be set in an area with a grid of tracks, paths and routes where controls are put on line feature junctions, so that the course cuts diagonally across blocks of wood-land.

Orienteers run on bearings on the orientated map as far as they can to hit the junctions knowing that they will be caught by a line feature either side if they are not accurate.

2. The aiming off strategy can also be built into this type of exercise whereby, if aiming at a control on a line feature like a path the competitor

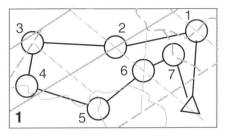

Fig 6.9: Cutting across blocks of woodland

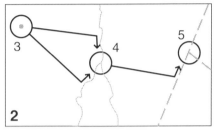

Fig 6.10: Aiming off

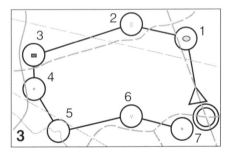

Fig 6.11: Compass and distance course

deliberately takes a bearing to one side so as to will know which way to turn on hitting the path.

3. A course can be set round line features with the object of running steadily, with controls placed just off the paths so that distance has to be measured accurately while running.

7 Heading for the hills: coming to terms with contours

As the summer months went by, orienteering played an increasing role in the Wood family leisure time. May and June are busy times in the orienteering calendar. Unfortunately it is always a busy time in schools too, so although on most weekends at least one of the family competed in a local Colour-Coded or Badge event, often it was as part of a shared car with other club members rather than as a family unit. However, Tuesday evening training sessions were usually a 'must', not just because they contributed significantly to the valuable reservoir of skills and physical fitness they were all building up but primarily because of the opportunity they gave to meet friends and talk about events past and future. The barbecue evenings and handicap events were special favourites.

The two major events in the British Orienteering calendar came a little too early for the family. The Jan Kjellström International Festival over Easter and the British Championships which closely follow it offer courses for all age groups and rotate round the 12 regions annually giving a variety of terrains and levels of competition. Unfortunately for the Woods, like the Scottish 6 Day Event which followed, both were in the far north and although camp sites, village hall and hostel accommodation were readily available, both the steep forests and long journeys eventually decided the family to wait a year when the Jan Kjellström moved to a seaside venue in the south west and the British Championships took place in the Woods' own region. Only Natalie was very disappointed. She had been winning events and fancied her chances in the British Championships, but both mother and father were concerned that too much success too early wasn't necessarily a good thing for the size of her head. They preferred that she should see orienteering as one of a group of fun activities, rather than the centrepiece of her existence.

However, Chris in particular was increasingly aware that there was still a big gap in their orienteering experience which would have to be addressed if they were to achieve more in the sport. Although Michael and Helen were quite happy to see orienteering as part of a recreational weekend scene and to do the minimum of training to make Sunday competitions relatively painless, they were now being drawn along by their children - Natalie because she liked winning, Samantha because she wanted to qualify with her friends for the Regional Junior Squad and for training camps in Scandinavia - and, if all went well a passport to the glamorous world of international competitions. Both Samantha and Chris had now moved into the Gold category in National Badge Events and were figuring strongly on Green Colour Coded courses, and in Chris' case sometimes Blue, but both were aware that their best results came on easy, well-pathed areas. Once contours reared their ugly head and navigation required reading detailed ground shapes, their confidence and performance quickly fell apart.

A joint decision therefore was made to combine a family camping holiday with a multi-day event in the Lake District in August. 5 competitions were on offer, all with a full range of courses and classes, all in different venues within 50km of the central camp site, and all on hilly areas offering a variety of contour challenges. The family kept to the same classes that they had entered in the Badge Event. Mum and Dad were quite happy to keep to short courses and to survive all 5 days rather than overstretching themselves and either failing to complete or finishing in a sea of exhaustion. The terrain for each event offered great variety from steep coniferous forest with rocks and rough brashings underfoot, to small areas of oak plantation on plateaux of rocky knolls and marshy depressions, and to open fell side with cropped grass underfoot making for fast running, but

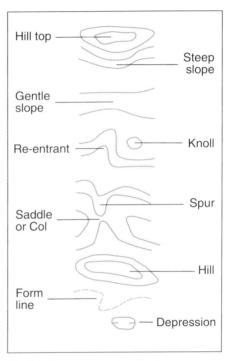

Fig 7.1: Common contour features

with only stone walls offering any clear handrails. The 1:15,000 maps reflected the complicated contour detail.

Good visibility on the fell areas meant that Michael's compass strategy could be very effective. By taking a series of bearings between obvious hills, valleys and rock features, he could simplify the navigation and leave fine map reading until the last hundred metres. Helen and Samantha had more trouble, relying much more heavily on walls and lines of marshes which had to take the place of the paths they were much more familiar with. In the forested areas lower visibility and undergrowth meant that 'reading the ground' became even more difficult and the key strategies became adjusting speed to difficulty and relocating quickly when lost. Apart from Natalie who once again was able to use a combinations of walls, speed and luck to sail round her course, all the family had more relocation practice than in the whole of their previous year's experience of orienteering put together - and not all of it wholly successful.

Chris perhaps was the most interesting case. After disasters on Days 1 and 2 when three twenty minute mistakes sent him way down the results list, he suddenly discovered on Day 3 that by running hard to obvious wall junctions and field corners on an area that was a mixture of scattered trees and open fell, he could then walk to the control with a combination of compass bearing and map reading and thereby make safe, if not perfect, progress. To his surprise, this

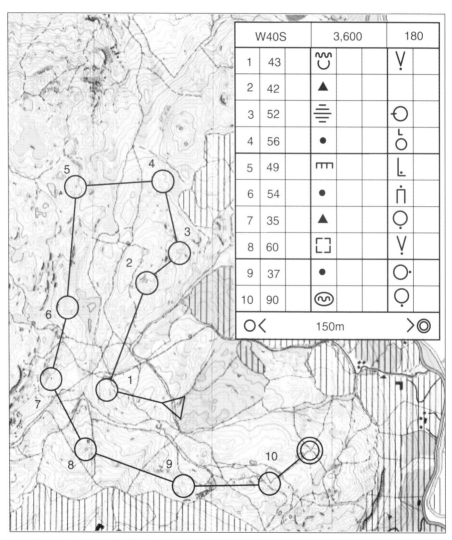

Fig 7.2: Helen's map for Day 4: a lunar landscape of rocky knolls, crags and ridges

Fig 7.3: Cragfoot 1.5m

technique took him to the head of the results list in M15 that day, his first win in a major event. However, his cumulative result was still well down the field.

The format of the event involved adding each day's result times together to provide a chasing start on the final Day 5. In this, each competitor started in cumulative time order based on the previous 4 days, the first past the finishing post being the winner.

Day 4 on an open fell above Ambleside saw some revival in the Woods' fortunes, though in this lunar landscape, few competitors moved with any speed or confidence. Sitting on a high vantage point near the fell top, the planner could see queues of walking orienteers converging on the few paths or marshy plateaux, before fanning out into the scatter of rocky knolls and rocky ridges to find the elusive control markers nestling in small niches, beside boulders or at the foot of crag steps.

On Day 5, Natalie was 3rd in the start order for W11, 3 minutes behind the leader, Samantha 15th, 14 minutes behind, Helen 10th, 20 minutes behind, Michael 6th, 10 minutes behind. Chris lay 9th, 11 minutes down. Because some competitors were very close in time and because of adrenalin produced by the competitive system, concentration and speed control are always vital in this type of event. Nor did the type of terrain help - a rolling area with scattered trees, rocky ridges and marshes and only the inevitable stone walls to provide reassuring hand-rails and relocation points.

Fig 7.4: Michael's technique on Day 5: knoll hopping towards an obvious attack point.

This time, it was Natalie who 'fell apart'. Catching the leader at control 3 and finding herself in the lead, her legs took over from her brain and she ran right past control 4 and almost off the map, before retracing her steps and recovering to finish 4th.

Helen walked, in her usual determined style, putting contact with map and ground before all else as rivals ran backwards and forwards around her. Much to her surprise she moved up to 6th - very much a tortoise triumphing over hares. Michael too played for safety, hopping from knoll to knoll on compass before 'bouncing off' obvious attack points into the controls. He felt very satisfied with his 4th place, in M45S. Samantha proceeded in fits and starts: a leg when ground and map made sense and the control leapt out at her would be followed by a leg

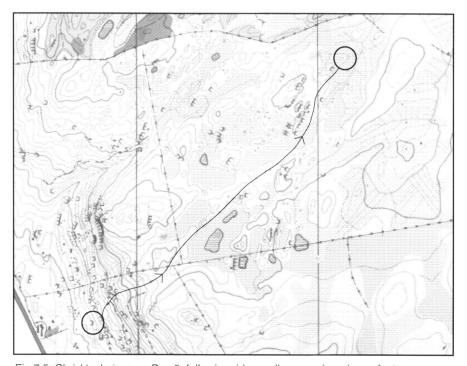

Fig 7.5: Chris' technique on Day 5: following ridge, valley, marsh and crag foot

in which she wandered from hillock to hillock peering behind each one before seeing a rival punching in front of her. 75% right and 25% wrong saw her finishing 14th, one better than her start position. Chris was the luckiest. Seeing that a long ridge ran straight towards his first control, a small marsh, he sprinted down it catching up the 8th competitor who, being a northerner, was well used to this type of orienteering. Running not far apart for the rest of the course trying to out-navigate each other, inevitably they helped each other inadvertently and one by one overtook those in front. More important from Chris' point of view was that contour orienteering suddenly began to make sense. As his rival followed ridge, valley, marsh and cliff foot, linking them up like line features between controls,

Chris grew in confidence, knowing for the first time that he could live with the best, and delighted with his final position of 4th and 2nd fastest time of the day. Nor did his performance go unnoticed. The Junior Squad coach was already putting an asterisk against the name of 'newcomer' Chris Wood.

The Woods returned home tired but not disheartened. They had completed a key phase of their orienteering education, and if they could now build on the experience, the whole orienteering world in all its variety lay waiting for them. If we can make an analogy with literature, before the Lake District Event their orienteering had been Enid Blyton: now they had been introduced to Shakespeare, and couldn't wait to sample more contour dramas.

Now let's look at contour orienteering in specific coaching terms.

Contours

More than a few orienteers in Britain have a phobia about those squiggly brown lines on the map and some tend just to ignore them. But you do so at your peril. Brown is the most important colour on the map. If you want to succeed in the detailed terrain of the Lake District, North Wales, Scotland or Scandinavia, then contour skills have to be mastered and practised to perfection.

A map is a two-dimensional representation of a three-dimensional environment and cartographers therefore use contours in order to give their maps the illusion of depth. An appreciation and understanding of contours is vital to good orienteering technique.

Contours are lines on the map which join together points on the ground of equal height. They enable the reader of the map to visualise the shape of the ground before he even sees it and, because the shape of the ground normally doesn't change, the orienteer can use this knowledge to his advantage.

On orienteering maps con-

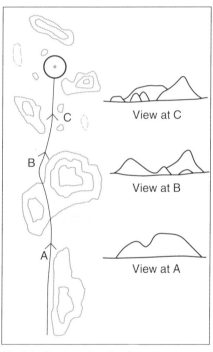

Fig 7.6: Contour visualisation

tours are usually drawn at 5 metre intervals (sometimes 2.5 metres on very flat areas) and the mapper tries to draw them in a way which will aid the running orienteer. This means that he will often 'help' the contour along by emphasising some features at the expense of others or by exaggerating contour forms to make the shape of the ground clearer.

Whilst marshes and streams may dry up in summer or become lakes and raging torrents in spring; when tracks and paths seem to appear and disappear with monotonous regularity and trees are felled and planted according to the forester's cycle of activity; when man is constantly changing the fixtures and fittings of the environment, the shape of the earth remains virtually constant. The best navigational technique, therefore, is one that recognises this truth and, ignoring the clutter left by man, concentrates on the shape of the ground alone.

Elite orienteers rarely use vegetation boundaries or vague man-made line features as handrails but instead rely upon ridges, re-entrants, hills and spurs to lead them towards the control. Good orienteers tend to be those that are most skilful in contour visualisation.

Contour visualisation is the ability to form a mental three-dimensional picture of the terrain from a detailed study of the map. It enables the runner to compare a mental image of the ground with the terrain around, and then to use this information to navigate into the control.

Contour visualisation can be trained, and even if the average orienteer's mental picture of the ground is not as detailed as that of an elite competitor, the fact that an orienteer is starting to navigate by ground shape, rather than path system or straight compass and

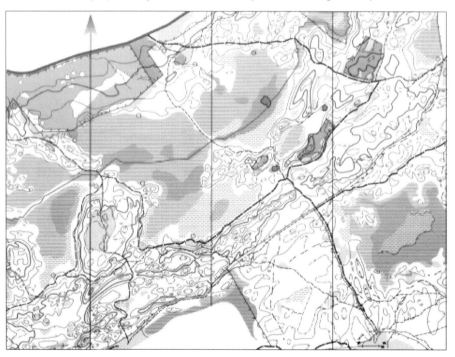

Fig 7.7: A Scottish map showing fine contour detail: which obvious features can be used to simplfy navigation?

pacing, means that bad mistakes will become less likely and navigational style is beginning to be built upon sound principles.

A 'contour navigator' isn't put off by felled areas, overgrown paths or new fences. As long as the ground fits the map there is no problem. In many Scandinavian events newly felled areas aren't shown on the map and nobody seems to worry!

Fig 7.6 shows a typical control area where a competitor would seek to form a clear mental picture of the exact pattern of hills and marshes before reaching the attack point. This information can then be used to steer the way into the control or to relocate easily if the marker is not found first time.

Contour awareness influ-

ences every other basic orienteering technique. Route choice is affected as unnecessary climb can now be avoided and contour handrails identified to guide the runner towards and into the control. Relocation is easier in heavily contoured areas, and plenty of contour detail in and around the control circle can make fine navigation much easier than merely relying on compass and pacing.

The supreme test of contour technique lies in the glaciated terrain of Scandinavia and parts of the Scottish Highlands where complicated contour detail is often combined with thick but runnable forest. Here two different but complementary contour techniques are needed. The first is map-to-ground technique; the second is ground-to-map.

In applying map-to-ground technique, the orienteer plans a route and then chooses predetermined checkpoints along the way, like hills and marshes, to confirm it. The terrain, is visualised before getting there and the orienteer mapreads ahead to keep the initiative rather than allow terrain or chance to dictate choices.

In ground-to-map technique the running orienteer looks for features on the ground which can be related to the map, and by doing this confirms that the direction is correct. Compass and distance work has to be accurate using this method.

It is important that, whichever technique is employed, the orienteer doesn't just simply run off in the general direction of the control hoping that features will turn up to keep the line right. For this reason,

Fig 7.8: Map to ground

map-to-ground technique should be considered as the basic and superior skill for most conditions of orienteering. Ground-to-map technique then becomes an important but secondary skill for use as a back-up or as

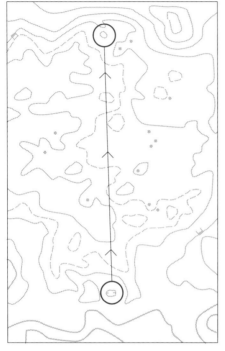

Fig 7.9: Ground to map

the basis for the continuous relocation and relocation-on-the-run techniques described in the previous chapter. In both cases, however, the good orienteer will be using contour features as the primary means of getting to the control with accurate compass work confirming direction.

Since contours are so important to good orienteering technique it is imperative that, right from the start, children and other newcomers to the sport are encouraged to see a map as a three-dimensional representation of the ground and not

simply as a plan view of interlinking paths and other man-made 'lines'.

The book Teaching *Orienteering* advocates that when introducing children to mapreading at school, their first maps of the classroom or gym should concentrate on the position and size of objects as well as lines of walls, windows and corridors. Swedish research has shown that even 6 year olds can appreciate the relationship between 3 dimensional objects.

Contour models in sand, wood or polystyrene can reinforce

Fig 7.10: Contour patterns

contour visualisation and when children are taken into real terrain for the first time they should be encouraged to identify and evaluate land shapes, even though they may only be in the early stages of handrail navigation.

With growing experience, children can be expected to learn to identify and name basic land shapes such as spurs and re-entrants, and to adapt their orienteering style according to the demands of geology and map detail. Some examples of different contour patterns are shown in fig 7.10.

There are many exercises to train and develop contour awareness and visualisation: following a contour on line courses; contour-only courses; map memory contour exercises and even simple practical mapping.

One excellent exercise is for orienteers to divide up into pairs with one orienteer putting out controls and then drawing a contour sketch map for the other to find. Another simpler version involves each of a pair hanging a marker on a control feature and then collecting the partner's marker. Accuracy has to be balanced against speed in trying to be the first back to the start. Practice at hanging out the controls on contour features when setting up training exercises can also provide valuable reinforcement.

Probably the biggest difference between British and Scandinavian orienteers is that Scandinavians navigate by contour features practically all the time. I was reminded of this recently when giving a lift in my car to a Swede in Scotland. As we drove through Achray Forest I was surprised to discover that, unlike a Brit who

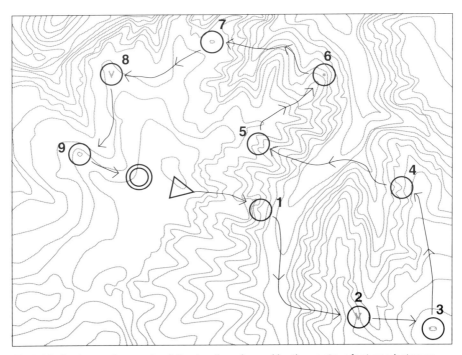

Fig 7.11: Contour-only exercise following lines formed by the contour features between controls

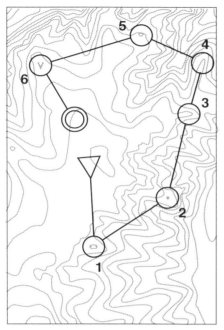

Fig 7.12: Fine contour-only exercise with controls close together to force concentration on ground shapes

would plot his progress by referring to the road bends or junctions with forest tracks along the way, Erik was plotting our progress on his orienteering map by reference to the hills and knolls beside the road!

As with the development of all orienteering skills, practice makes perfect. So, whether you are doing physical or technical training, look ahead on the map and confirm your position by contour shapes. That way you will be a real orienteer rather than just a trail runner. Orienteering at the higher levels is all about seeing the skelton of terrain beneath the skin of map detail and using this to decide routes and navigational strategies.

Contour visualisation

8 It's all in the mind

The lack of confidence which had so inhibited the Wood family's performance early on in the Lake District 5 Day Event and the sudden improvement which resulted from increased self confidence gave them all a lot to think about once back home. Once past the introduction stage, so many mistakes in this, as in earlier competitions, had resulted not so much from lack of technical experience but from failure to apply knowledge in the right places and at the right times. Often it was due to lack of concentration, before the start, on meeting a friend in the forest, running too fast and taking risks through over confidence, or in Sam's case in particular, day-dreaming when tired.

Natalie's mistake on the final day was totally due to over confidence and lack of concentration. Both parents had missed the first control after joking at the start with friends and dashing off into the forest aimlessly, while Chris' success in the chasing start had been mainly due to concentrating hard on doing the right things so that he didn't lose ground on his rival. Some orienteers react positively to this type of head-to-head competition. Others switch off when they find themselves running alongside a rival and get badly lost if he or she makes a mistake. Chasing starts, like relays and international competitions can bring out the best and worst in competitors, though the successful ones are usually those that concentrate totally on their own performance during the race and only think about position and time when they look at the results board afterwards.

Although most sports psychology tends to be applied at elite levels, there is much which applies equally well at all levels and in a sport like orienteering where decisions are often made under stress, it is important that even beginners realise the key roles played by concentration, a clear head and the ability to control anxiety levels. As the Woods had already realised, every orienteer has to be calm at the start and in a positive, concentrated frame of mind. Too much adrenalin and too much stress and the first control is missed, which then starts a chain reaction of loss of confidence, anxiety and more mistakes. They had also found that as their fitness increased they were less likely to get into oxygen debt and make mistakes through lack of oxygen to the brain. Michael in particular tried hard to make the difficult decisions on easy parts of a course and not while staggering up a steep hill.

They had also learnt that it was important to have a personal race-day routine. In fact, each member of the family extracted a different element from the 5 Days' experience and tried to build it into their orienteering style. After the next club training evening they sat down to share ideas with their friends. As a result, Chris and Samantha started to keep training diaries. Natalie resolved to slow down near controls, Helen decided to try some relaxation tapes recommended to her by a friend and resolved to get a bit fitter by jogging, cycling and swimming and Michael set himself some goals for the rest of the year, the main one being to hit the first control cleanly in 3 consecutive events. Chris and Sam also collected competition analysis sheets from the club coach and decided to do some work at diagnosing their weaknesses and devising training plans to correct them. These they clipped into the training diary with each competition map showing routes and mistakes, thereby providing a useful record upon which to build preparation programmes in the future.

So bearing the Woods' experience in mind let's now take a closer look at the psychology of orienteering.

The psychology of orienteering

Johnny Nilsson, a Swedish coach and research psychologist, once introduced an international coaching seminar with the statement that orienteering is 90% psychology.

This was an intentional exaggeration, yet it is certainly true that many experienced orienteers who have mastered all the basic skills still fail to realise their potential and perform poorly in important competitions. In fact, as Johnny Nilsson was emphasising, a strong psychological thread runs right through orienteering technique and its application. If it is the 'natural sport for the thinking runner' then the thinking must direct the running and not vice versa.

There are two broad psychological areas which we need to consider:

Concentration: More than half of the competition mistakes involve

Fig 8.1: Concentration: "am I leaving the control in the right direction?"

being put off by other people. Concentration thus means the application of intelligence and mental control so as to use the right skills effectively at the right time, and to control situations which may distract or derail the competitor.

Devising warm-up procedures which produce the right degree of concentration and arousal at the start of an event, and maintaining concentration throughout the whole course of a race are therefore vital

Fig 8.2: Concentration through to the finish

psychological areas. Some competitors try to maintain concentration every moment of the course; others prefer to "switch on and off" according to the difficulty of the navigation.

Self-confidence: Specific mental training can be done to develop personal self-confidence and belief in your ability to perform consistently to the limit of individual potential. Above all else, the orienteer needs to stay calm and confident, avoiding over-reaction to external stimuli (panic decisions). It is necessary to think positively, have supreme self-discipline and the ability to build on success.

Training routines can involve relaxation training, the visualisation of good practice, and mental control drills. With experience, some aspects of this conditioning can be introduced into the warm-up.

Elite athletes work hard on these psychological techniques within their training programmes and many swear by particular systems or the influence of coaching gurus. However, the way the human mind works is no simple matter to understand, especially when coping with the pressure and stress of sporting competition. It would be irresponsible and dangerous for me to play the part of the sports psychologist. Even a little reading can be a dangerous thing so I suggest that, if this an area which interests you, you consider one of the excellent Level 1, 2 and 3 courses on Mental Training, Training for Peak Performance, and Mind and Matter, put on at regional centres by the National Coaching Foundation.

Having said that, many successful sports people, including Carol McNeill one of Britain's most successful competitors, give high priority in their preparation programmes to mental preparation, visualisation and other techniques for producing a positive attitude on the big occasion.

I would, however, like to draw out several psychological threads for you to consider.

Goal setting: Goals establish personal targets to aim for which can provide motivation and diagnostic feedback on what else needs to be done to do even better. Competition results make the only effective judgement on training programmes. Competition goals should as far as possible be within your own capabilities to achieve (e.g. less than 5 minutes of mistakes in a race) rather than partly dependent on others (e.g. winning the British Championship). It's a good idea to discuss your goals with a coach or friend as long as they remain yours, and not the product of unrealistic pressures.

Personal weaknesses and blocks: Every sports performer has weaknesses. The important thing is to identify these and then to work at making them strengths. This means filling in event analysis sheets to diagnose problems, devising training strategies to cure them and working hard to build up technical confidence. Sometimes, the cure needs lateral thinking. One orienteer who regularly missed the first control eventually solved the problem by concentrating hard on the second!

Preparation routines: A preparation routine before every competition is vital. The mere fact of going through a regular proven routine is psychologically reassuring and can build up the concentration and positive thoughts the orienteer needs at the start of a race.

Such a routine is an intensely personal matter, and what works for one may be disastrous for another. Some orienteers seek personal

Fig 8.3: Mental training helps to cope with pressure

contact before the off, others prefer to build up concentration alone.

Coping strategies: Coping strategies can be devised for many technical areas of orienteering. An example is playing for safety after a mistake rather than taking risks to make up lost time. Another is taking safe routes towards the end of a long race to cope with the effects of fatigue on concentration. Some orienteers take a quick look at the whole course on an easy path run early on; others may use easy sections to relax concentration before tightening up once in the forest again. My son, Steve, not only talks to himself during a race to maintain concentration on the right things but always does something positive to switch on concentration,

Performance	Good	Fair	Poor
Concentration before the start			
Route planning			
Control entry			
Control exit			
Rough map reading			
Detailed map reading			
Rough compass bearing			
Accurate compass bearing			
Rough pace counting			
Map memory			
Map understanding			
Terrain understanding			
Checking features			
Independence of other runners			

Loss of time	Leg/control number									
	1	2	3	4	5	6	7	8	9	10
Ran too fast										
Orienteered too slow										
Underestimated difficulty										
Took a chance										
Didn't have a good attack feature										
Didn't check off enough features										
Poor route choice										
Didn't follow the planned route										
Lost concentration										
Followed other runners										
Other runners followed you										
Disturbed by other runners										
Not used to the map										
Not used to the terrain										
Didn't read the control description										
Was tired										
Thought the map was poor										
Read the map poorly										
Poor compass bearing										
Poor judge of distance										

Fig 8.4: Event analysis and table of techniques used

like checking the compass bearing.

It is just as mistaken to say: "I can never cope with the big race" as it is to say: "I can't cope with exams or interviews". First of all, know yourself: then develop coping strategies for vulnerable areas while training hard to strengthen them, then build up a competition style which plays to your strengths (e.g.

Fig 8.5: Smooth control discipline saves time. Punch quickly but confidently and then check the direction out with the compass

look for fast running routes if you are a fast runner, etc.) and finally accept that everyone finds it difficult to cope with pressure but that it's possible to train mental skills and powers as well as physical.

Training under pressure

Some element of pressure training is good during the pre-peak training period. Mass start, head-to-head races force competitors to concentrate, hill intervals with a mental calculation at the top can identify problems associated with oxygen debt, and map-memory events in which each leg has to be memorised at the previous control can help build up visualisation and concentration.

Finally, I should stress that timing is very much a psychological area in orienteering, as in most other sports: knowing which skills to use when, and co-ordinating them in an efficient orienteering rhythm which becomes subconscious. A tennis player doesn't consciously think about leg, arm and body positions when serving in a match; similarly the orienteer should be slotting together map, compass, pacing and other routines in a race without really thinking about it.

This depends on a lot of training and competition experience. Traffic light exercises with coarse, careful and fine orienteering sections can help here as well as training courses in which very long and very short legs are interspersed, and multi-purpose courses demanding emphasis on different skills at different points.

As a last thought, remember that in psychology as in all training areas, it comes down to the individual. Beware especially of being misled by an admired role model. Most experts orienteer automatically without thinking consciously about techniques. They sometimes find it difficult to see orienteering in beginner terms. When a World

Champion says 'I never pace' it is easy to forget that many hours were probably spent pacing as a youngster until judgement of distance no longer relied on it.

So listen to advice but, with experience, work out strategies which suit you and then practise and apply them consistently in competition situations.

It's all in the mind

9 Not just a sport: more a way of life

The days moved on, summer holidays ended and for Natalie, Samantha and Chris it was back to school, and tales of holiday adventures to share with friends. The Lake District orienteering saga attracted willing listeners, some of whom were keen to try this new sport themselves.

Sam was surprised when her Physical Education teacher began to take an active interest and asked if there were any local events coming up where she could take a look at orienteering herself and perhaps take some of the interested children along too. That evening Sam looked at the fixture list in the club magazine and saw that a Come and Try It event was being organised on a local common on the last Sunday of September and that club members were being asked to help. The Woods decided to offer their services and the three children agreed to help any school beginners on the day and to try to help their teacher start a school club if enough children were interested afterwards.

The following morning Sam and Chris opened their mail to find that both were invited to join a Regional Junior Squad course at a local Outdoor Education Centre the week before the Come and Try It, providing another boost to their orienteering motivation which now seemed to be going into overdrive. So that Natalie didn't feel left out, Helen suggested that she help her teacher draw a new accurate black and white map of her school and grounds which would make the orienteering in geography lessons more interesting and appeal to Natalie's liking for art and design.

Inevitably, both parents were drawn into their children's enthusiasms. Father Michael found himself driving Sam and Chris to the Bowers Centre for the weekend course. Helen set to, providing polyester film, 5H pencils and drawing pens, compass and measuring instruments for Natalie's mapping venture, as well as joining Sam on her training runs round local footpaths. Both ended up organising the start for the Come and Try It event. Chris too was asked by the planner to help put out controls while Sam volunteered to give help at the master maps, which for this introductory event were set up near the registration cars so that courses could be chosen and then copied up carefully well before the start.

The last piece of the autumn orienteering jigsaw came with a letter to both schools advertising a British Schools Championships in November. The Wood children had already heard about this event from club friends, but because it was based on school teams, the age group competitions were team centred, and neither of their schools had so far been deeply involved in the orienteering scene. They had dismissed the project as unrealistic at present but perhaps something to be considered for the future. However, ideas were now being driven by events, and a lot could happen in two months. If a number of children were motivated by the Come and Try It event, and if the school teacher could be persuaded to take them to two or three local events, and if the Wood children could give some training help in the meantime, then perhaps a school team could be entered and a new orienteering chapter opened up.

Fig 9.1: Schools championships

The British Schools Championships are held at a different venue each year, usually near a big city and with cheap floor accommodation provided in a local school for the Saturday night. With a training event the day before and perhaps 1500 children taking part from all over the British Isles, it was both a social occasion and a big adventure in which all three Wood children were desperate to be involved. This year the Championships were being held in a big country park in the Midlands so the orienteering wouldn't be too difficult nor the journey too long. For Natalie's primary school there were 4 in a team and for Chris and Sam 9, so there was quite a lot of missionary work to be done.

Things never go as perfectly as planned and the Woods' autumn experience included traumas as well as triumphs. Overall however, positive dominated over negative. Two hundred assorted children, mums, dads and friends took part in the Come and Try It event and of these twenty joined the club and twelve converts decided to form a school club. Natalie was not so lucky. Only four 10 year olds came along from her own school, and their parents insisted on doing the course with them, inevitably with Dad doing the map reading.

The Squad Course was a great success. Thirty 13-18 year olds took part from all over the region and Sam and Chris enjoyed both the Traffic Light Exercise in Bishops Wood and the afternoon activities which included canoeing, caving and abseiling under the tuition of centre instructors. The Night Event which followed was not such a positive experience. Neither had orienteered in the dark before, and although the courses were easy and all on paths, they found their hand torches put them at a distinct disadvantage against the more experienced youngsters who had invested in sets of head lights, some of them with halogen bulbs.

Sunday centred on a multi-technique course, after which they analysed their mistakes with guidance from coaches and discussed training plans for the following year. These included for both the goal of getting in the region's team for the Inter Regional Junior Championships to be held in Scotland in June of the following year. Both youngsters slept soundly in the back of Michael's car on the journey back home - as the parents were to learn with experience - a sure sign of a successful weekend.

Natalie's map-making was a story of highs and lows. Initial enthusiasm turned to despair when she discovered the maths involved in taking precise bearings and measurements, adjusting grid to magnetic north, and plotting every tree and goal post exactly. However, once she discovered that the school plan given her by her teacher was pretty accurate and that pacing worked, she soon took off, and with assistance from teacher and parents, went on to map the small area of wooded parkland on the school's southern edge at a scale of 1:2000. She particularly enjoyed copying up each day's survey on her neat master copy. In a few weeks she was able to draw it all up carefully with a Rotring pen onto a piece of polyester drafting film, and with the help of Letraset and skilful penwork gave the map a "professional appearance" for photocopying. The final version in photocopy form is shown on page 24. It provided many hours of useful orienteering activity which, to her great surprise, produced 6 new converts and the nucleus of a school team for the British Championships, if not this year, perhaps next.

Chris and Sam did get to the Schools Championship, Chris in the 16 age class, Samantha in the 14, this event being unique in the orienteering calendar in providing a course for every age year from 11 to 18. Both finished in the first 10, but with the other team members finishing in the 30's and 40's, their school finished well down. However, the new converts had enjoyed the weekend and made many new friends. The new school club was now off the ground and their teacher was determined that next year it would be different. As well as regular

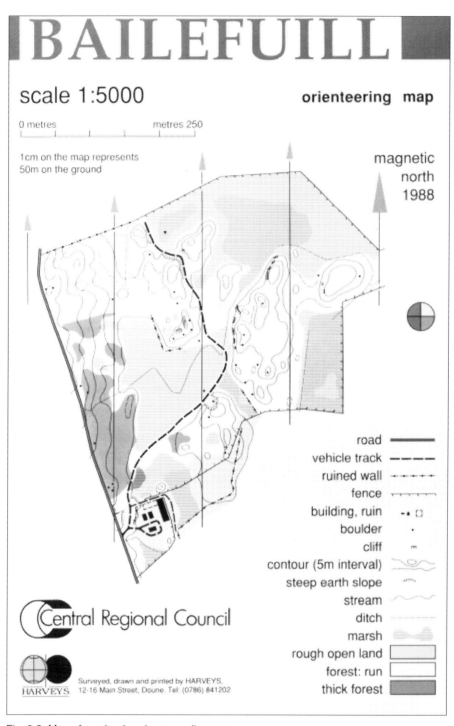

Fig. 9.2: Map of a school and surrounding area

trips to local events, Sam was already talking about a School Inter-House Event, a summer camping weekend, a competition for places in next year's teams and the introduction of some orienteering into the Physical Education curriculum, which is how Chris and Sam now followed Natalie into school site mapping with the ignominy of having to ask their younger sister for advice. There are a number of interlinked threads of interest in all this experience.

Introduction to orienteering: The Come and Try It event and the children's school experiences raised again the question central to the Wood family's introduction to orienteering. What is the best way to introduce the sport?

Natalie's converts had come from a teacher-controlled introduction on the school site and child-centred mini-activities on Natalie's new map. The three children taken round their short course by their parents could have learnt from the experience, but because their parents did the map reading and made all the decisions, the children were robbed of the essential experience offered by orienteering - to navigate on one's own in a mini-wilderness. Some who came to the Come and Try It event had had basic instruction, some were already proficient with maps and compasses in non-orienteering terms, some had no background and no idea what to expect, some arrived with more experienced helpers. Helen and Michael gave basic help at the start to those who were obviously at sea, but it was clear to them that many had not read the explanation sheets given out at registration, that some had entered courses beyond their capabilities, and that in this sink or swim situation many would get lost and turned off the sport for good, or simply follow others and end up doing a recreational walk rather than completing a navigational challenge.

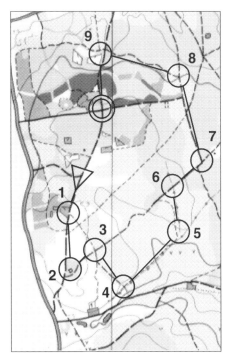

Fig 9.3: Come-and-Try-It Event: short yellow course

Samantha's approach illustrated one form of good practice. She had once again persuaded Javindar to come along, this time with another friend Sundip. Before starting, she taught them both how to orientate their maps with the compass and saw to it, that, although they would take part together with one control card, each had a map. She then checked that they had copied up their Orange course accurately and once they were off in the right direction, hovered behind them only interfering when they were obviously making a bad mistake or needing help. Once they were over half way round the course and gaining in confidence, she left them to it and retraced her footsteps to help others who were having problems. In so doing she noticed some parents using the same approach with young children or in some cases a family group going round together with the children doing the map reading.

Chris' approach was different. He had persuaded three of the School Cross-Country team to give orienteering a try and directed them to the Red course. He went over their course with them beforehand persuading them to draw in red the paths and tracks they would actually follow, even where these safe routes meant a considerable diversion from the straight line. Although all three started a minute apart he realised that they would probably converge as a group and compete against one another, but hopefully, this way they would be running hard and not getting too badly lost as long as they kept to their predetermined routes. Another group of friends on mountain bikes adopted the same tactic and so much enjoyed the experience that they decided to plan their own mountain bike courses on maps in future and to build in the same route choice challenges as orienteering.

Getting started in orienteering, as we noted at the beginning of the Wood story, means enjoying the first experience, keeping to handrails, and not getting badly lost. Within these parameters, so much depends on age, fitness, background and expectations. A fit athlete wants to run rather than map read at a walk, a cyclist wants to cycle. So in these terms, Chris' approach was a good one. Samantha's friends however, wanted to get round the course safely, so her controlled safety-first approach, like that of parents with young children, was a sound one. In some ways, the Helens and Michaels of the world present the biggest problem - how to combine interesting challenging orienteering with fading fitness and limited opportunities to train. But now we're back to the starting theme of our book. We've come full circle.

We should not forget too, Chris' part in helping to put out controls. To his surprise, this took much more care and concentration than expected, even though each point was marked by a small red tag checked by planner and controller. Hanging a control accurately in an empty forest is more difficult than navigating to a marker already in position - and as Chris found there is nothing better than planning courses and hanging markers accurately to tighten up map reading and terrain visualisation.

Mapping: As well as forming an orienteering area of expertise and interest in its own right, and one which provides the sport with its most important resource, mapping can also be an excellent method of training map reading and navigational precision. Even the surveying and drawing of simple school maps builds up these skills, and what's more, encourages the orienteer to see navigation through the mapper's eyes.

Even Natalie's short experience, as well as providing a lot of interest and satisfaction, built up her capacity to judge the relationship between objects in the school grounds, reinforced her concept of scale, developed her compass and distance judgements skills (which had let her down in the Lake District) and forced her to map read in very precise terms. Most elite orienteers have included some mapping in their orienteering education and in talking about locating the marker within the control circle, some will say "I mapped the area in my head so that I knew exactly which knoll the marker was on".

Team competitions: In orienteering, as in many other sports, team competitions can be great motivators. In looking for and training new members for a school team, Sam and Chris were developing the sport within their school in a very positive way, though the short time scale in which they were working meant that they were risking throwing newcomers in at the deep end without the experience to cope. Although planners of schools events, including championships, try to contain mistakes with catching features behind controls and to keep courses relatively easy, there are always a few competitors each year who get badly lost and demotivated. Natalie's approach and time scale with her own

Fig 9.4: A group walk can be fun: but who's doing the map reading?

school were perhaps more effective in the long term.

The whole family were to discover before the end of their second year in orienteering that Team Relays, Team Score Events, Inter Club Competitions and even Mountain Team Score Events (sometimes called Rogaines) can also be powerful motivators at club level.

Social factors: These play a powerful part in every sport and particularly with Juniors. The British Schools weekend, the new School Club, the involvement of Chris' cycling friends, the club evenings and the Regional Squad weekends were building up a complex network of friendships, and rivalries.

The Squad weekend in particular had included party games (some related

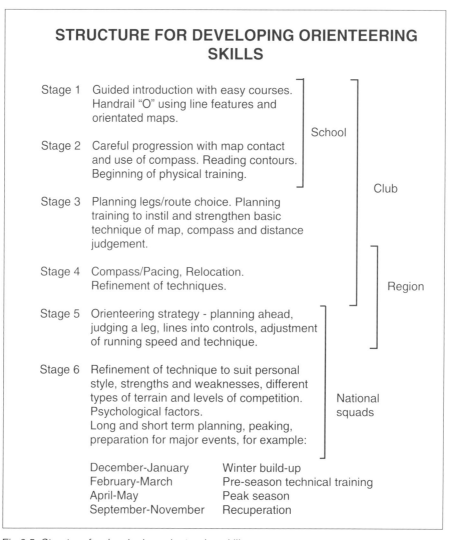

STRUCTURE FOR DEVELOPING ORIENTEERING SKILLS

Stage 1   Guided introduction with easy courses. Handrail "O" using line features and orientated maps.

Stage 2   Careful progression with map contact and use of compass. Reading contours. Beginning of physical training.

School

Club

Stage 3   Planning legs/route choice. Planning training to instil and strengthen basic technique of map, compass and distance judgement.

Stage 4   Compass/Pacing, Relocation. Refinement of techniques.

Region

Stage 5   Orienteering strategy - planning ahead, judging a leg, lines into controls, adjustment of running speed and technique.

Stage 6   Refinement of technique to suit personal style, strengths and weaknesses, different types of terrain and levels of competition. Psychological factors.
Long and short term planning, peaking, preparation for major events, for example:

National squads

December-January	Winter build-up
February-March	Pre-season technical training
April-May	Peak season
September-November	Recuperation

Fig 9.5: Structure for developing orienteering skills

to orienteering) as well as providing a relaxed environment for experiences to be exchanged, plans made for the future and relationships to develop. Plans were already afoot for a Christmas party and a training camp in Norway the following summer for which funds had to be raised in the months before by the sale of refreshments at events, raffles and the like. Samantha was in her element - squad weekends were now fixed points in her diary and an increasing number of her friendships were now developing within the sport. Helen and Michael too had enjoyed helping at the event and were themselves finding new attractions in the sport as well as new friends. They had already decided to organise and plan the Come and Try It event the following year, to build in more pre-instruction and help, and to include a string course for very young children. Helen had decided to find out more about teaching orienteering and had already signed up for a one day course leading to qualification as a BOF Instructor.

Chris and Sam were now moving onto a steeper development path than the rest of the family, one which would take them as far as their potential and motivation would allow.

Although the objective of the Regional Squad was to produce more competent and confident orienteers rather than to look for future international performers, inevitably its members were taught the principles of physical and technical training and encouraged to plan and keep records of personal training programmes. Initially, these were built round other school sports and activities including academic work and, especially in 14-year-old Sam's case, involved only a basic foundation of physical conditioning and skills training, built largely round club and squad training plus the occasional extended training course further a field.

However, in 16-year-old Chris' case, the training plan decided upon between him and the Regional Coach included training which was specific to orienteering, as well as goals related to an improvement in particular technical skills.

Although the principles behind training programmes and their planning and implementation relate mainly to orienteers determined to climb the performance ladder, many training principles (as with psychological guidance) can apply equally well at more modest levels, though with much reduced intensity. We will therefore conclude this chapter with a detailed examination of the planning of orienteering training programmes, bearing in mind that for the Helens and Michaels of the orienteering world much of the advice and information will have more relevance to an understanding of their children's progress in the sport rather than to their own orienteering performance.

Planning training

Improvement in sports performance doesn't come by dabbling in training theory or just going to the odd course or two. In addition, though you may have mastered every step in the skills progression, if you don't keep the components locked together into an orienteering style which you sharpen up with practice, you won't be a consistent performer. And then of course, there is that vital matter of producing the right performance when it really matters. Champion orienteers are the ones who produce their best on the day it counts.

Here we will cover personal training programmes, short and long term planning, and preparing for optimum performance in important events. Detail on physical training is dealt with in a later chapter.

Carol McNeill, World Veteran Cup winner 1994, is Britain's supreme exponent of tailoring training to specific goals and producing a great performance at the time of her choosing rather than at the whim of chance.

As an elite orienteer her orienteering year was planned with training patterns geared to key competition phases of about a month to six weeks each. The winter training phase of steady terrain running built up basic fitness and was followed by a shorter period of quality running and technical input before the competition phase of races interspersed with specific tune-ups and recovery sessions. Within this pattern, she advocates a balance of easy and hard days and weeks and argues that training programmes must be geared to an individual's lifestyle, goals, ability and motivation to train, with the right balance of speed, strength, stamina and flexibility work. As a dynamic W50 she still applies these principles with great success.

None of this is contentious. I would add, however, that training programmes must be judged on outputs, i.e. competition results and not on inputs, i.e. volume of training. One athlete can achieve on 6 hours training a week what another achieves on 12 hours, and if the average orienteer sees three training sessions a week plus the weekend event as a maximum, then it is entirely reasonable to look at this pattern and to see how it can be used to achieve the maximum training effect. Figure 9.7 shows an example of a year plan suggested to a student.

This is built around exams, selection and anticipated representative races. The training content, which we can assume for this level of orienteer was discussed with a coach, is fitted into a 5-hour training week during the winter and 4 hours during the summer. It is flexible and is adapted according to competition results, training feedback and general health, condition and motivation/attitude. As much priority is given to rest days as to hard days.

Sometimes an orienteer will put a great deal of thought into a personal programme, follow it through conscientiously, and then find that the anticipated improvement or success doesn't come. There can be many reasons for this. Human beings are complicated machines. For most of us, sport is only one part of our lives, and problems with work, family or health can wreak havoc with a training load which puts demands on a full lifestyle. Training schedules must always be built into lifestyles.

So if you're ill, upset or tired,

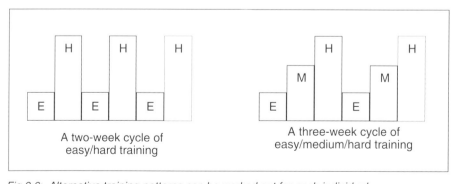

A two-week cycle of easy/hard training

A three-week cycle of easy/medium/hard training

Fig 9.6: Alternative training patterns can be worked out for each individual

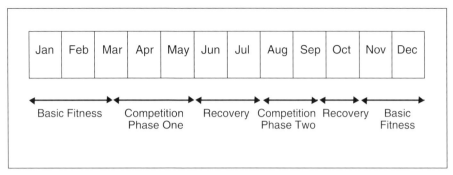

| Jan | Feb | Mar | Apr | May | Jun | Jul | Aug | Sep | Oct | Nov | Dec |

Basic Fitness   Competition Phase One   Recovery   Competition Phase Two   Recovery   Basic Fitness

Fig 9.7: Training year plan

then rest and adapt your programme accordingly. If things aren't going well try to talk to a friend or mentor (there are never enough coaches to go round, even in Scandinavia). Perhaps the results aren't coming in test races or on test training circuits, or on the positive side you may have a new bright idea for training. In both cases, discuss it and be flexible. Don't forget too, that improvement takes time. Success rarely comes overnight.

Some important principles

Confidence breeds confidence, and, of course, the reverse is true too. It's difficult to break a string of disappointing performances, and once problems have been diag-nosed, it may be that selected local events have to be used to try out coping strategies and concentration drills as well as specific training exercises.

As already stressed in Chapter 8, *Mind over matter*, carefully planned preparation procedures for events are vital. All the benefits of a systematic training build-up will be lost if the competitor gets to the start late or in an anxious, flustered state.

At every level, it is important that an orienteer follows a specific plan before major competitions for the previous 24 hours or even longer. Indeed, it may well be that, once proven, it should be followed for all competition so that it becomes habit and psychologically reassuring.

Useful points to emphasise here are:

a) Find out as much as possible about the competition area well beforehand. Run in similar areas and with similar maps in the weeks before, and if possible, at the same time of day as the competition race.

b) Plan your journey to the event well in advance and make sure you leave plenty of time. Write down a 24-hour timetable leading up to the race.

c) If it is likely to be very hot or very cold, get experience of running in similar temperatures. This may include getting used to taking liquid on board during the course of your training runs.

d) Check all your clothing/equipment and have spares ready.

e) Make sure you know the race procedure and start method, and that you have your own system well prepared. Know where you are going to carry your control descriptions and punch card.

f) Establish a routine warm-up system, including mental preparation, to produce the right balance of concentration and arousal at the start.

g) Ignore the opposition until you look at the results board.

h) Warm down carefully and analyse the race afterwards, drawing your routes onto your map, noting the time lost through mistakes and establishing why as well as what went wrong.

The training diary

Most of these issues, together with the diagnosis of personal weaknesses were discussed in the section on psychology. I would like to repeat something I said then: the consummate athlete identifies his or her weaknesses and makes them personal strengths". Perfect orienteering runs are extremely rare, but mistakes give vital coaching feedback. (See page 80 for event analysis sheets.) You should positively use events for training. Sports watches make it easy to time every leg and by comparing with friends of similar capability, it's easy to identify patterns of weaknesses and strengths. While using training to improve weak areas, in major competitions you should play to your strengths, for example, if you are a fast runner but weak technically, take path routes to obvious attack points.

Training files and diaries are also important in the planning process. For elite orienteers they should include all the relevant information including type of training, time/distance, rest periods, sleep patterns and athlete reaction, and they should be filed with the map record to provide a comprehensive data base upon which training programmes can be designed. For instance, if a championship race goes well, repeat the preparation pattern before it and refine it over the years so that it becomes a psychologically reassuring personal system.

Many orienteers may say that this type of planned training isn't for them, and that they see a pattern of regular Sunday events with a club training run once a week and the occasional social run as fulfilling all they want from orienteering. There is, of course, nothing wrong with this approach which probably reflects the attitude of the majority of recreational sportspeople. All we are saying here is that as an orienteer you will want more satisfaction from the sport and that if you want to maximise your personal potential to perform better, then planned training procedures are the most effective way of achieving improvement. Fundamentally it comes back to what you personally want from orienteering and your motivation, ambitions and available time and energy.

Conclusions

Perhaps I could conclude with three further observations:

Britain may not have Scandinavian forests but it does have an equable climate, a long running tradition and a good orienteering event structure. Many of our new breed of elite orienteers who

Training Diary | **Actual Training**

Name: Jonathon Duncan M19
Club: Walton Chasers

Date	Training Description (Planned)	Time	Session	High	Medium	Low	Type of Training	Running Surface	Strength Training	Mobility Training	Technical Training	Other Activities	Daily Total	Comments on Daily Training
6	Brown Course Colour Coded Event - Cromford - physical area	55 mins	1	✓			Comp	Rough			✓	Warm down	55 min	First race for some time. Really enjoyed it. Went well technically and physically. Think 7 was 15-1.
7														Rest day after hard weekend
8	9km speed/strength session	60 mins	2		✓		Int	Grass				Warm up and down	60 mins	5 x 1km intervals round school field 3.11/3.07/3.06 3.12/3.15. V.6 session - felt good but tired. Strong wind towards end
9	12km steady to hard run	55 mins	3	✓	✓		Long run	Roads/Paths	✓			Warm up/d	55 mins	Steady 4km. Towers run with map. Felt heavy. Pushed hard up hills and over the tops. Not much speed.
10	Fartlek session at medium effort	50 mins	4		✓		Fart	Road/Patio	✓			Warm up/d	50 min	Feeling much better - more speed on hills but getting there! Still not 100%
11														Rest day. Travel a/to school to Surrey
12	Compass/Pacing Exercise 100 mins on Leith Hill + Short Race	100 mins	5	✓	✓		C/P					Warm up/d	100 min	C/P not so good - missing controls to left! 2 sessions ruined by mistakes in race

| Week No: 10 | Total per Week | | 5 | 3hrs | 2½hrs | | | | 1½bbl | | 1 hr | 60 mins | 12hrs Total |
| Month: March | Total per Period | | 49 | 15hrs | 25hrs | 9hrs | | | 15hrs 5hrs | | 2½hrs | 15hrs 5hrs | 50hrs Total |

Assessment of week 5 4 3 2 1

General Comments
A good weeks training with some quality physical work - esp the interval session. Not overtraining very well technically - despite some positive legs in the training race, too many inconsistencies. Ankle niggles at times.

Comments on the Planned Training:
The physical side has been going well. I'm stronger than last year and should make the County Cross Country Team for the All England. Leith British Champs so early 9 need more tech work. Dodgy ankle is holding up.

Coach's Comments on the Planned Training:
I'm very pleased with the way you're shaping up to the plan worked out last November. We agreed then to work on running strength/speed and to bring in more tech. training in March - which is what you're doing.

Coach's Comments on Actual Training:
At this cold time of year - pay more attention to mobility exercise. In your warm up routines - top with speed sessions. Don't do intervals to absolute exhaustion - perhaps you should have stopped at 4 in the Tues session. You need now to get race speed and technique back into synch. Squad weekends will help.

If you make the County Team you'll have achieved one of your goals for the year.

Fig 9.8: Training diary filled in by an M19 competitor

1994 SQUAD YEAR PLANNER

Name *Jonathon Duncan* M19.

WK. ENDING		EVENT	LOCATION	PHASE	TRAINING / COMMENTS
January	1			Stamina / Strength Building	Long. Runs up to 90 mins — terrain running. Fell Races. No serious racing.
	2				
	8				
	9				
	15	Squad Day	Cannock Chase		Introduce intervals within
	16				Hard. medium - easy structure.
	22				
	23				
	29				
	30	C.C. Event	Sutton Park		
February	5	Squad ⎫		↓	Introduce more speed here -
	6	weekend ⎬	Coniston		try 2× Interval sessions per week
	12			More Speed	School Cross Country Races
	13				for speed and Card/Vasc Fitness.
	19			↓	One or two events to assess
	20	Noc CC Event	Sherwood		technique
	26			Introduce Tech Tr	Use squad weekends for tech.
	27	Help Nat Event II	Hawksmoor		Hang controls - for tech. training.
March	5	Reg. Squad Day	Hawksmoor	↓ Tech at Racing Speed	Use events now to develop
	6	English Schools X/C			technique at racing speed.
	12				If ankle causing trouble - wear
	13	Rehearsal Race	?	↓	brace.
	19	BOF Champs ⎫			
	20	BOF Champs ⎬	Goodwood	Competition Phase	Work on mistakes highlighted
	26				by BOF champs
	27				
April	2	JK ⎫	Hereford		
	3	JK ⎬			Work on mental preparation.
	9				Try to keep clear of injuries
	10				Confidence in technique
	16				important here. Fitness level
	17	Nat Event II	Yorkshire		should be high.
	23				
	24				
	30	Selection Races ⎫	Scotland		Try to peak for these races despite
May	1	for JWOC ⎬		↓	the difficult time !
	7				After short rest, try to keep
	8			'A Level Exams	fitness going during exam period
	14				through easy running before building
	15				up for JWOC and summer
	21				international competitions in late June/
	22				early July.
	28			↓	If JWOC fails make the
	29				European Inter. in Sept a goal.

In Events Column Use ....   ✷ ✷ Peak   ✷ Major   (N) Not Important   / Continued ....

Fig 9.9: Year planner designed for a squad member

TRAINING LOG   Name: Sam Wood   Month: January   Year: 1994

(W 17)

Day	Intensity: Maximum	Intensity: High	Intensity: Moderate	Intensity: Low	Strength (snow)	Strength (aerobics)	Other	Orienteering Tech	Competition	Training Type: Running: Terrain	Training Type: Running: Track / Rd.	Training Type: Running: Paths	Cycling	Circuit Training	Swimming	Training Breaks: Rest	Training Breaks: Injury	Training Breaks: Illness	Training Time: Session 1	Training Time: Session 2	Mental Training	Comments
1			✓									✓							30			Jacobs ladder, easy. 5km
2																		✓				COLD
3																		✓				
4			✓							✓									30			Easy on Common. 6km.
5	✓	✓								✓									45			Hard up Hills on Common 8km.
6	✓															✓						
7			✓								✓								30			Mod. Rd. run. (6km)
8		✓							✓	✓									38	30		1st Club Champs. 4.7km (5P40). Run Home 5km.
9			✓								✓								40			Jacobs Ladder + Rd. 7km.
10																✓						
11		✓								✓									38			Terrain on Common 6.5km.
12			✓								✓								30			Rd. 6km.
13	✓					✓						✓							35			J. Ladder Fartlek. 2mins max. 2mins r
14		✓								✓		✓							60			Terrain / Path on Common 10km
15																✓						
16			✓								✓								25			Wildwood Rd.
17	✓	✓				✓					✓			✓					30	40		1. Hard Gym. 2. Rd. with Club. 8
18			✓								✓								30			Easy Rd. 6km, tired.
19																✓						
20	✓					✓						✓							50			Hill Int. 1.13, 1.0, .58, .56, HARD.
21		✓						✓		✓									75			O'course on Common 10km.
22			✓							✓									36			Terrain 6km.
23																✓						
24	✓	✓				✓					✓			✓					35	42		1. V. hard W.C.H gym 2. Rd run. 2mins slower [illegible]
25																✓						
26			✓								✓								30			Fast 6km Rd.
27	✓					✓				✓									60			Hill Int, 1.03, .54, .51, 1.0, .55 + Ru
28		✓								✓		✓							60			Fairly hard terrain + J. Ladder.
29		✓							✓	✓		✓							65	20		C. Woods. Blue 6.1km, tough. E.N. 67mins. + 3km collect
30																✓						
31		✓									✓			✓					30	38		1. [illegible]. Gym. 2. 8km. Rd. run, faster!
Number of sessions	5	10	9	-	-	5	-	1	2	10	9	6	-	3	-	7	-	2				
Total time Hrs.	4	6	6			4		1	2	6	6	4		1								

% of total training time

Comments for Junior:

Good that you took it easy after your Cold.

After that a good quality month of hard work which will lay a good foundation for summer competitions.

Fig 9.10: Samantha's training log

have progressed through the system from age ten to twenty-five have learnt and developed all the basic techniques in British terrain and then applied them consistently and effectively all over the world. This has meant using our terrain imaginatively with contour-only maps, corridor and window courses and the like, and it has meant practising basics like compass, pacing and visualisation even when easy British forests have invited a fast thrash round paths or tracks. It has also meant getting involved in allied running areas like fell and cross-country races to give a break from orienteering and to build up running speed and competitive drive.

Sometimes, too, it has meant restricting races to perhaps ten or so a year. 100-minute winning times in elite races put the orienteer in almost the same category as marathon runners when it comes to physical and mental wear and tear, and to take part in an event every week could be folly. Planning training and competition can also mean accepting criticism for not competing every week and accepting some poor results in the interests of using events as training. Long-term success is often at the expense of short-term glory, especially at junior levels.

Junior training needs exceptional care, especially during growth spurts between thirteen and sixteen when the bone/muscle structure can be developing rapidly. Girls in particular need special support during adolescence when physical changes and other pressures on time and attention can easily push

sport aside, especially when success becomes more elusive. In fact, for growing young orienteers, a performance-based competition structure like the colour-coded model is much more appropriate than one based on ages. Human beings both mature and grow old at differing rates but the physical damage from over training and over racing children can be irreversible and the demotivating effect on slow developers of discovering that they were not the world beaters they first thought, is well documented in all sports and is certainly not unknown in orienteering, particularly on the girls' side. For young juniors, therefore, training should be one play activity amongst many other sport-related activities.

Training diaries should not be considered until sixteen plus, and although dramatic physical improvement is possible in the seventeen to twenty year age span with correctly designed training programmes, junior coaching strategy should always be medium to long term with consistent performance in the early to mid-twenties as the goal, and a balance struck between physical and technical development.

Although it is good to have role models and to learn from the experts, never copy other people's schedules. If 'Orienteering for the Thinking Runner' means anything, it means making your own decisions. Former double world champion Oyvin Thon defined orienteering as a "sport in which the competitor decides where and how fast to run". The same principle applies to planning training.

10 Physical training

The months moved on from winter into spring. For the Woods, orienteering continued on its merry rambling way. Britain is one of the few countries where the orienteering fixture list is uninterrupted by winter weather, though some of the local events the family attended were bizarre in the extreme as fog, rain, ice and snow transformed familiar landscapes overnight. So while Scandinavians and East Europeans took to their skis for Ski Orienteering, the Woods, like most other British orienteers accepted cold hands, wet feet and misted spectacles as all part of the orienteering challenge. Sometimes, as fog turned to bright sunlight on a wooded hillside, an event provided experiences to treasure; on other occasions the hot bath back at home and the map post mortems proved more pleasurable than the battle with the elements which had preceded them.

Winter too is a time of thinking and planning for the summer, both in training and competition terms. Helen and Michael were looking enviously towards the Scottish 6 Day Event in August, Samantha and Chris had ambitions to be selected for a Junior Squad Training Camp in Sweden, and the whole family had pencilled in the British Championships and Jan Kjellström Trophy dates as well as forms of orienteering new to them like the Harvester Inter Club All Night Relay, and Regional Score Event Championship. Meanwhile, Helen found herself volunteered for a Club Social Committee and Michael found himself increasingly involved in giving help and advice to the teachers trying to develop orienteering in the children's schools. Both continued to keep fit.

The children's interest in orienteering too was developing further. Natalie still yearned for her school to enter a team in the British Schools Championships and now gained a lot of enjoyment in planning orienteering games for her small group of converts on her new school map. Her mapping experience had deepened her interest in drawing and design work and she was more than happy to help her father in his first mapping attempts at her brother's school, this time for a 5-colour 1:5000 map which would be printed professionally. Samantha had decided to work really conscientiously at a winter training programme devised with the help of one of the club's best young orienteers, who had become an important role model for her. She now ran with the school cross-country team one day a week, ran the path circuit near home on another and tried to fit in as many technical training days as possible at weekends. Sometimes she used a Sunday event for training, concentrating on a particular skill like compass or route choice depending on terrain and quality of course. She had highlighted the important competitions she wanted to do well in on her year plan and hoped that now she was entering the W15 age class, she might stand an outside chance of being selected for a summer squad training course. Helen sometimes worried about her daughter running in the countryside alone and at first worked up the energy to go with her. Soon, however she realised that Sam was developing into an extremely confident and single minded young woman who was determined to do her own thing, and so she settled for the role of confidante and sounding board for ideas when things didn't go quite right.

Fig 10.1: Confident running in the countryside

Chris had become attracted to the athletic side of orienteering. To his surprise the fitness built up through orienteering won him a place in the School Cross-Country Running Team, and, sparked off by a 4th place in the School Inter House Championship, he became member of the local athletic club. Every Tuesday evening he joined a pack run round the estate roads behind the village and soon found that he was more than holding his own with accomplished cross-country and 1500 metre runners. Mountain biking too had won him over, and often on a Saturday when there was no orienteering event, he would be riding hard with a group of friends on tracks up hill and down dale trying to keep contact with the local 1:25,000 Ordnance Survey map. The orienteering club had a winter handicap race each year run over 5 kilometres with the help of a black and white map. Based on his age as a first year M17 with relative inexperience, he was given a 3 minute lead on the scratch runners. To everyone's surprise, he not only overtook all the assorted Mums, Dads, children and older runners in front but held most of his advantage to the finish to win by a clear 2 minutes. The new superfit Chris was obviously now a running force to reckon with, but could he make his new speed and strength pay in orienteering terms?

Logic would suggest that a faster Chris would take the junior orienteering world by storm that summer, but it is obviously vital that orienteers run in the right direction. 30 seconds gained over a kilometre by fast running can easily be lost by poor map reading near the control. Every orienteer, no matter how experienced, must keep speed and map reading in tandem. Running too fast for technique, especially with young male orienteers like Chris, is a frequent cause of competition traumas. Success for Chris in the important competitions to come would require a lot of self-discipline and running training with map in hand rather than an athletic relay baton. The other important factor in orienteering is that it demands running of a rather special type. If the basic elements of fitness are speed, strength, stamina and suppleness, then orienteering requires specific strengths and flexibility not needed by the marathon or track runner.

We will now look at physical training for orienteering in detail and relate it to the training programmes discussed in the previous chapter. Once again, much of this material applies most to the elite end of the sport, but if 'elite' is defined as anyone working hard to fulfil their potential, then many orienteers of all ages and abilities will find the analysis which follows of interest.

Training for physical fitness

Although it is vital for success that every orienteer should choose and keep to the right route, all other things being equal, it will be the orienteer who travels the fastest who will win the race. In fact, the ultimate test of all training programmes is the time which goes up on the results board.

Speed does not simply depend on cardiovascular running fitness. Speed for the orienteer means running through marshes, zig-zagging through boulder fields, fighting through thick forest, driving up and down steep ridges and hurdling over fallen branches.

Orienteering running is a skill in itself. It demands strong thighs, knees and ankles, a flexible upper body, high knee lift and a driving, flexible stride. The style of the marathon runner or the floating stride of the middle-distance runner will not work in the forest. Even the experienced cross-country runner soon finds his natural rhythm is

Fig 10.2: Hurdling orienteering style

disrupted by the rough forest floor with its rocks and brashings. An elite orienteer running on flat surfaces may appear to be over-striding in an un-economical fashion, while his cousin the track athlete will lose his customary relaxed style in the forest as he uses unnecessary energy struggling for balance and drive in unfamiliar surroundings.

Orienteering running is a skill that can be learned like any other, but it requires the right attention to

Fig 10.3: Look before you leap

the specific demands of 'terrain style'. Physical training for orienteering, therefore is about more than simply achieving road running fitness.

There is another aspect of orienteering running which I need to touch on before turning to specific training tips. Marathon runners run aerobically. That is to say they exist for the course of the race on oxygen generated by the heart and lungs without running into oxygen debt; it is oxygen debt that produces awkward waste products like lactic acid

and reduces physical and mental performances. For many years it was considered that orienteers should attempt to run aerobically too in order to prevent oxygen debt inhibiting their decision-making. Now, however, research seems to indicate that the modern elite orienteers, running to the limit of their physical powers, can spend up to a third of the race in oxygen debt.

Every time the elite orienteer crosses a ridge or drives through a marsh he tips over the aerobic threshold and then recovers on easy

Fig 10.4: Liz Dunn and Gill Hale race it out

sections later (rather like a cross-country runner putting on a series of bursts to break an opponent). Indeed, in international relay races, where there is very often direct head-to-head racing, orienteers sometimes deliberately put in these running bursts in order to confuse their opponents and induce them to make mistakes.

There is another side to the coin though, and orienteers must

Fig 10.5: Steve Hale: supreme terrain runner

learn to recognise the symptoms of oxygen debt and try not to make navigational decisions at those moments in the race when they might be suffering. For this reason many elite orienteers try to read the whole of their course early on in the race; ideally during an easy section (such as a path run) where they can make their basic route choice decisions before their mental performance is degraded by the onset of oxygen debt.

By now I am sure that many

of you will be thinking that what I have just said is more applicable to running in Scandinavia than in Britain for, I hear you say, the path and track systems of most British forests allow fast aerobic running between controls without recourse to direct terrain running. (I can still remember, in the early days of British orienteering, Gordon Pirie setting off to run one of my 10km courses in 40 minutes just to prove that track running fitness could pay off in orienteering terms.) However, it is surprising how quick the straight

Fig 10.6: Jon Musgrave: super fit, long striding and strong

line can be, even in British forests, for the fast, fit and determined orienteer.

On undulating areas like Cannock Chase in the Midlands of

England, I have seen generations of young elite orienteers slowly begin to discover that, with terrain fitness and strength, straight is best. They often take some convincing but I have done this by comparing the times taken to cover 1km over terrain, paths and tracks. I remember to this day a 13-year-old Walton Chaser (Walton Chasers is the local orienteering club) by the name of Steven Hale being slower than his cross-country runner friend on paths and tracks, yet leaving his rival for dead when they entered terrain.

So, accepting that the supreme orienteer should be strong, flexible, fast, long-striding - a 'driver' rather than a 'floater' - with excellent cardiovascular fitness to push back the aerobic threshold as far as possible, what type of training programme should the coach and athlete devise to produce this orienteering paragon?

The problem in answering that question is that the orienteers reading this chapter will all be starting from different levels of physical condition and, given the nature of our sport, will vary enormously in age. It would be irresponsible of me to start suggesting universal schedules because every programme must be designed and adapted for the individual. This is true for every sport. What I would like to do, however, is lay down certain guiding principles and then to toss out a few training ideas for consideration.

Perhaps I should say right from the start that, if orienteering is a sport for the thinking runner and if we live in a country which combines the ideal climate, countryside and, moreover, tradition to encourage running activities (and I believe it is and we do,) then it is a source of constant surprise to me that more British orienteering clubs have not ploughed the rich furrow of running ideas which are not only appropriate to orienteering but which would also make winter training evenings so much more interesting that simply meeting together for a road run.

Seven guiding principles

Long, slow running: Long, slow running may be both socially and psychologically reassuring but if you can carry on a normal conversation whilst jogging along a road then you are not producing the overloading effect which will lead to an increased

Fig 10.7: Bounding: learning from the experts

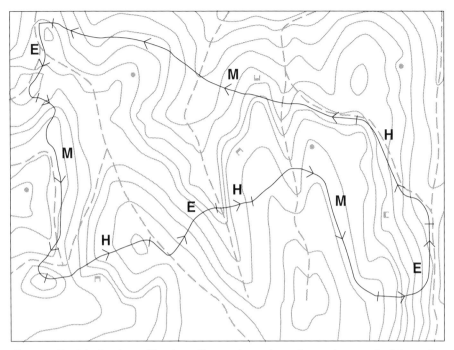

Fig 10.8: Fartlek. Sections of hard, medium and easy intensity running on a fartlek session. There is no need to take a map and the route need not be planned in advance.

level of fitness. It is not the type of running that you are likely to be doing in an orienteering event, and because it takes a long time (and orienteers are usually busy people) it is not time-efficient. If long, slow running has any place in orienteering training it is when 'long' represents the amount of time you normally spend out on an orienteering course and 'slow' equates to the sort of intensity of running that you are likely to devote to the average orienteering event.

Hills: Orienteers spend a lot of time running up and down hills. Your training should reflect this. Hill running can produce dramatic improvements in cardio-vascular fitness. In most parts of Britain it is not difficult to locate a 200m hill. Go out and find one. Try running hard up your hill for 30 seconds (it doesn't have to be very steep - 1 in 10 will do), put down some form of marker and then trot back down to where you started. See how many times you can repeat this and still hit the marker. If you haven't warmed up properly you will probably find you overshoot at first and then, after another two or three repeats, you will start to drop back.

This exercise can provide the basis for the number of hill intervals you build into your training schedule. You should also try to start running on the downhill recovery sections. Another good idea is to run a hilly circuit ironing out the speed differences on the ups and downs. But whether you are running uphill or downhill, it is amazing how much time you can gain in an event if you simply keep running slowly rather than always stopping to walk.

Fartlek: Fartlek (a Swedish word meaning 'speed play') running sessions can be more fun than straight running and are quite appropriate to the type of running that most of us do in an orienteering event. Draw a line on a map showing fast and slow sections, or try the follow-my-leader system in group training (which helps the slowest runner as well as the fastest). Even the monotony of a run around the housing estate can be broken up by lamppost sprints or hill surges. Orienteering training needs either this type of input or some straightforward interval runs (i.e. a series of fast runs interspersed with recovery jogs).

Gym work: In the winter months the gymnasium can be put to good use with programmes designed to build up specific muscle groups as well as general flexibility sessions (e.g. circuit training for thighs, stomach etc. as described in *The Coaching Collection)* see Appendix H. Swedish groups spend a lot of time in the gym when the winter snows put their forest out of bounds for training.

Terrain running: There is simply no substitute for running in orienteering terrain or on terrain-like surfaces (e.g. grass verges rather than roads). In an ideal world we would carry out most of our physical orienteering training in the same place we practice our technical skills - in the forest.

Combine physical training with technique drills: Technical training and physical training are not mutually exclusive. Technical training can be given a physical element with benefits accruing to both areas. For example, intervals based on pair route choice exercises; or interval training in which pairs run hard to a catching feature and then walk or jog to a more subtle control feature for the recovery period; or follow-my-leader runs between controls with the follower trying to make up a time deficit.

Don't forget to warm up/down. Warming up before an exercise period and warming down afterwards are essential if injury, boredom and over-training are not to become part of your training schedule too. Flexibility and rest are also important, and above all, do not train if you are suffering from an infection.

Training ideas

Indoor exercises. As an alternative to circuit training why not set up indoor relay runs based on map games (e.g. transferring information from a master map or memorising map detail?) As well as livening up the dull winter training periods, these exercises can be useful vehicles for illustrating the effect that oxygen can have on decision making.

Map line running. Simply draw a line of given length on a map and run on it, pushing hard on the easy technical or physical sections and recovering on the hard ones. Much of the Scandinavian physical conditioning is built on this principle. Or simply plan a course to test a particular technique or series of techniques.

It is important to make sure

Fig 10.9: Line running round Drumlanrig: fast or slow according to technical difficulty

that the line is not too long (perhaps 60 minutes if you are thinking of taking that long in your next event) and that you employ hard running and not merely jogging. Some Swedes I know even extend this exercise to cover night training, claiming that running this way at night (with headlamps on, I hasten to add) improves their relaxation, style and confidence.

Interval O: This comprises a series of short orienteering sections interspersed with recovery jogs on paths. Pairs alternate and compare notes, reversing legs on the return run.

Slalom O: Zig-zag taped runs through forest (up and down) with the run being timed. This tests both speed and agility.

Hashing: Most orienteers have heard of hashing: many of you will have tried it. Those that have will be able to testify to its benefits. It is essentially a stylised form of the old paper-chase (hare-and-hounds) in which the planner lays down a sawdust course in woodland or open countryside. which the chasing pack have to follow. By a series of checks and false trails the speed of the chasing pack is regulated so that the slower runners find that they are engaged in an elaborate fartlek exercise with fast legs (when they are on the right trail) interspersing with slow ones (when they are not). The group is kept together by slipping in short cuts for the slower runners at loops in the course.

Handicap races: Club handicap races, either straight racing or round an orienteering course, are always

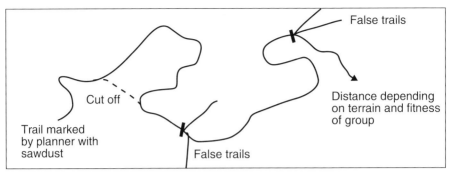

False trails

Distance depending
on terrain and fitness
of group

Cut off

Trail marked
by planner with
sawdust

False trails

Fig 10.10: Hashing

an excellent training vehicle and a good way of fostering club spirit.

Before I finish this section on physical training, a few ancillary words of advice:

Interval training is not recommended for under-17's or over-50's. Even for those ages in between it can be a very draining form of training. It should be hedged with easy or rest days.

Running schedules should not suddenly be increased by more than 20% at a time and the principle of following a hard day with an easy one (or a hard week with an easy one) is generally a good thing.

Training with someone else can be more fun than training alone. Orienteers, like all sportspeople, learn and gain an awful lot from sharing ideas and experiences.

Research has shown that a certain amount of physical stress and arousal can actually help the decision-making process but it is all too easy to tip over the edge into fatigue, which then undermines concentration and decisiveness.

Above all, the orienteering dimension makes running more varied and enjoyable. Try some of the ideas here and see for yourself.

Setting out a training exercise

11 Putting it together in racing terms

Despite - or perhaps because of his ambitions - Chris had a mixed summer season. A 5 minute mistake on control 1 of Day 1 of the Jan Kjellström Trophy Event saw him running even faster to catch up time - leading to another 5 minute mistake at control 2. He then overreacted by cutting back to a jogging pace for leg 3 and saw his chances and hopes for a place in the first three evaporate. It was hardly surprising that his Day 2 run completely lacked confidence as he proceeded in fits and starts to finish in 20th place overall.

Nevertheless, Chris talked to the Regional Coach who advised him to build up his confidence on low key local events before the British Championships in May. This was a flat well pathed area in the Midlands and despite another mistake early on his course, Chris was able to make his speed pay and to his delight finished 3rd. In the Relay event the following day he ran first leg for his club and again allowed 'his legs to drive his brain'. Staying with the leading pack for the first half of the course, he began to visualise himself running down the finishing lane in the lead, and started to push along the pace from the front - with minimum concentration. The inevitable happened, a missed path junction, panicky relocation on a fence corner and 3 minutes lost. He handed over a disappointing 6th.

There were peaks as well as troughs. A fine run on the first leg of the Junior Inter Club Night Relay, his first serious venture in night orienteering, two wins in his age class to help his club reach the semi-final of the Inter Club knock out cup, and most pleasing of all, selection for a British Orienteering Federation training course for promising young orienteers taking place in Sweden. This Scandinavian experience played a significant part in Chris' orienteering development. Not only did he have to slow down and develop an orienteering rhythm in the heavily detailed forests of marsh and rock, but, even more important, the highly developed competitive system in Sweden raised his sights about what was possible in this challenging sport. Inevitably he made mistakes, but even with good runs, he finished well behind his Swedish counterparts.

After a reasonable run in a Junior Relay, he sat down afterwards to talk to

Fig 11.1: Relay change over

members of the winning Swedish team. He saw from their map routes that, although they made as many mistakes as himself, these could be measured in seconds rather than minutes. He also noted how they used lines of marshes and ridges to simplify navigation and followed terrain lines into controls. He also learnt that after a mistake it was important to take the next leg even more carefully rather than racing to catch up time which usually resulted in another mistake. When Björn, the captain of the winning team, suggested that they might write to each other and perhaps visit each others' homes the following year, Chris needed no second invitation. He had already decided that this could be the path to the exciting world of international orienteering and despite the training demands and dedication this might require, he was determined to give it a go. Like Steven Hale, Britain's World Championship medal winner in 1993, Chris had learnt from his mistakes on this first visit to Sweden, and having identified his weaknesses he was now determined to make them his strengths.

Samantha's season followed a more even path. Her thoughtful attitude to training and calm approach to major competitions meant that, unlike her brother, she performed consistently in all her peak races, finishing 4th in the Jan Kjellström and 5th in the British Championships. She also became a rock solid 2nd leg relay runner for the club and in both Inter Club knock out rounds won her class. On the basis of these results and a 3rd place in the Inter Regional Junior Champion-ships she too was selected for a training course for young orienteers, this time in the Highlands of Scotland. Her determination and motivation now equalled her brother's, and following his example, she was soon writing to contacts he provided, looking for her own pen friend, and hopefully a trip to Sweden herself in the following year.

Helen and Michael too had had a taste of night orienteering in the B class of the Harvester All Night Relay - an annual competition for club teams. However, the pressures here were those of keeping map contact and finding the elusive controls with the flickering head lights they had borrowed for the occasion. The word 'race' didn't seem a relevant one for their performance.

Chris and Samantha, however, were now taking important steps towards a form of orienteering which was as different from the local events in which they had started as downhill ski racing is from the turns and traverses of recreational skiing. Representative competitions for club, region or country involve head to head competition with pressures and demands all of their own. If the rewards in performance and excitement were enormous so would be the demands on training and nervous energy.

We'll finish the formal part of the Wood family story now with an examination of orienteering racing in its various forms and the most effective ways of preparing for it.

Fig 11.2: Head to head

Orienteering racing

In describing and discussing pure orienteering skills, we have stressed individual decision making, concentration and the importance of shutting out distractions presented by other competitors. There are however types of orienteering which introduce a "head to head" factor and thereby require a different approach to the techniques we have so far discussed.

By orienteering *racing* I mean all those types of orienteering in which orienteers are competing in the forest against others in a direct sense. This includes relays, chasing starts, international and other representative races in which all competitors are on the same course, as well as the new spectator/media versions of high-speed pressure orienteering like short distance orienteering and sprint orienteering. Since short distance is now included in world championships, the techniques I go on to describe will no doubt receive more attention in the future.

Let's look at some typical tactics employed in a relay mass start. Although there are course variations which emphasise the need for technical caution, most runners try to stay with the pack rather than try breaking away, very much in the style of cycle racing. Many elite competitors navigate

Fig 11.3: The fastest sprinter can make running speed tell

much more 'ground to map' than they would in a normal competition where the slightly slower tempo and lack of psychological pressure allows the orienteer to plan ahead with a map to ground strategy that is

safer but marginally slower.

Runners also tend to keep a wider peripheral vision so that they are aware of the movements of other competitors, and it isn't uncommon for running bursts and psychological ploys to be used to 'derail' and 'burn off' opponents. I remember hearing a young Swede in a Nordic Championship relay describe how he "kicked with two controls to go because I knew that I had the shorter 'split' towards the end of the race and could therefore burn off my Finnish rival".

Similarly, in a chasing start or head-to-head international race, it is not enough to get to the front and then relax into safety first orienteering, because faster orienteers may be behind and with everyone on the same course, hanging on and following become easier. This may mean the fastest sprinter winning rather than the best orienteer.

Speeded-up navigation

Short distance orienteering and sprint orienteering are designed to speed up navigation so that head-on competition generates small mistakes and heightens excitement for spectator or TV viewer. These forms of orienteering can also produce a first-past-the-post winner. The comparison that comes to mind is downhill skiing where the fastest competitor is at the limit of technique but must maintain sufficient control to keep on course.

The Norwegian men's relay team in the 1989 World Championships provided a supreme example of fast relay running to the limit without serious mistakes when they maintained a 2-minute differential between themselves and the chasing Swedish team for three of the four legs. On the last leg of the women's' relay, Sweden's Marita Skogum showed the same self-control under extreme, psychological pressure from the chasing Maria

Fig 11.4: Steve Palmer running into the finish

Galikova of Czechoslovakia. In a different way, the British men's team success in winning silver medals in the 1993 relay relied on two supreme exponents on the racing art, Steve Palmer and Steve Hale, outracing their opponents in catching up 9 places. Like Chris, both had combined orienteering and cross-country running as juniors.

Make running speed tell

In races of this sort, the orienteer must be flexible enough to take short cuts like aiming off for the head of the pack after a small mistake, and must be prepared to make running speed tell, as when the pack gather for the kill at the end of a first leg of a relay. On the other hand, the basic skills must be there like bedrock. A downhill skier may take a risky line but the bodyweight distribution will still have to be spot-on or a fall will result. Similarly, an orienteer may cut a corner by taking a direct line through a thicket but unless firmly glued to map and compass, the pack may be lost for good.

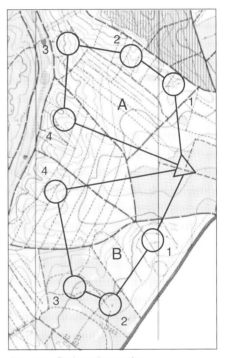

Fig 11.5: Sprint orienteering

Accepting therefore that racing technique demands navigation at maximum speed in a direct head-to-head competition situation, let's look now at appropriate training exercises. It is fair to say that many of them provide enjoyable orienteer-

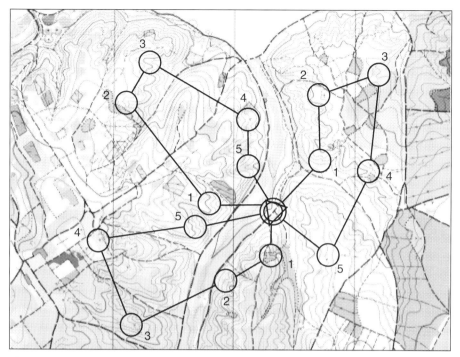

Fig 11.6: Mass start clover leaf relay

ing activity in their own right. I have found all of them sure winners on club summer training evenings.

Sprint knock-out event: This can be organised on a round by round knockout principle and spread over a series of evenings, or a head-on elimination race can be used to get down to the final four or eight.

A figure-of-8 course with 2km loops can give competitor and spectator progress feedback as well as building up the psychological pressures. Two or four runners can compete together with first back past the post the winner, though purists may object to four runners taking the loops in different directions for reasons of absolute fairness.

Runner A runs loop A followed by B; runner B vice versa. In the 4-man variation A runs clockwise first, B runs B clockwise first, C runs A anti-clockwise first, D runs B anti-clockwise first and so on.

Mass start cloverleaf relay: This is similar to sprint orienteering except that groups of runners run the loops in different sequences, so that although the head to head competition pressures are there, opponents change in the course of the race.

The courses should be balanced for time, though each loop can be given a different technical content to help runners diagnose their weaknesses.

Handicap race: Several courses are planned with a common start/ finish and competitors are allocated to them by ability, speed and age. A mass start means that first back will be the winner.

Chasing start race: A short

distance qualification race or score event can provide the start order which can either be at pre-determined time intervals or those produced by the qualification race. The danger with the latter is that long gaps can destroy the competitive nature of the exercise.

Punching relay: Teams of two or three, relay-style, with legs of 500m to 1km. The objective is to practice punching the control card efficiently. A short mental test at the end of each leg can drive home the effect of oxygen debt on decision-making!

Team score event: Teams of two, three of four split up the controls between them, the first complete team back wins.

Norwegian map memory event: A good way of using a small area intensively. Each leg has to be memorised from a map section hung at the control. Too much speed and too little concentration means steps have to be retraced.

Shadow training in pairs: One orienteer monitors another's technique or tries to outrun the other. There can be many variations depending on whether pressure, reassurance or coaching feedback are required.

Bergman intervals: Fast running

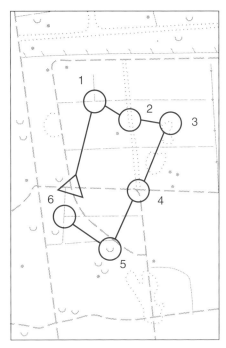

Fig 11.7: A punching relay can be a very simple course

to easy attack point then jog recovery section to control and so on.

Pursuit O: Hanging tapes in pairs: one tries to catch up a given time interval on the other on a series of pre-planned legs.

These exercises are all competitive and great fun. Finally it should be restated that team and

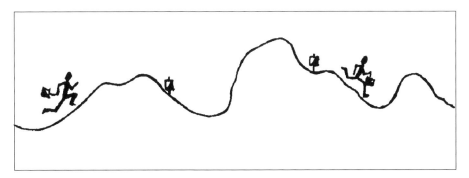

Fig 11.8: Pursuit orienteering

11	12	13	14	15	16	17	18	19	20
Thicket S end	Fence end	Camp fire	Copse SE side	Path bend	Path end	Path bend	Depression N end	Tap	Copse
15 pts	15 pts	15 pts	15 pts	15 pts	20 pts	20 pts	20 pts	20 pts	20 pts

1	2	3	4	5	6	7	8	9	10
Pond	Mast	Path end	Path bend	Tap	Statue	Hill top	Tap	Wood corner	Ditch bend
5 pts	5 pts	5 pts	5 pts	5 pts	10 pts	10 pts	10 pts	10 pts	10 pts

Fig 11.9: Team score event

relay races can be excellent for motivation and team spirit both in club and school, as Chris and Sam had found. Team relays and club competitions are a powerful factor in the success of the Swedish club system.

12 Into the future

Time has now moved on. It's ten years since the Woods tackled their first Permanent Orienteering Course and now Helen and Michael are venerable founts of wisdom in Club and community. They both compete regularly but tend to pick events in runnable forests or with proven planners and to eschew long Sunday morning drives on weekends away, unless for a championship or special occasion. Michael is now a rather ponderous M55 and Helen prefers to compete W45 though W50 is beckoning.

Michael's early retirement from work allows him more time for exercise and he tries to get in two or three easy runs a week with the dog, while Helen now works part time and runs regularly to keeps fit, also playing badminton at ladies sports sessions at the local Sports Centre. They look after and catalogue the club's stock of orienteering equipment which is kept in one of the spare bedrooms left by the departure of the children, and once a year they co-plan a local event as well as organising the club Christmas handicap and helping newcomers on club evenings. Michael is also a qualified Grade II Controller. Helen qualified as a Level One coach some five years ago and still helps with club training and girls' coaching on the occasional Regional Squad weekend. She usually finishes in the top 2 or 3 of her age group in local events. Both she and Michael now compete on A courses though Michael finds it difficult to keep fit and injury free for the longer men's courses. Although neither feels that they have reached their maximum in the sport in competitive terms, orienteering has brought a lot of new experiences and friends to their lives both in Britain and abroad, and as they pass into middle age, they can't imagine life without the orienteering dimension.

As for the children, Natalie is in her first year at University reading for a degree in Art and Design. As a junior she had promised much and had quickly achieved Regional Squad status as well as running cross-country for school and county. But Natalie has remained a girl of many enthusiasms and interests - painting, music, school work and friends all made demands on her time, and running for pleasure and fitness was easier to fit into her busy life style than orienteering.

She still orienteers recreationally and has joined the university club, where she sometimes helps its secretary, Samantha's old school friend Javindar, in attracting new members, but most weekends she is off fell-running or walking in the hills with her new boyfriend. She is looking forward to competing with him in the Karrimor Mountain Marathon Score Class in Scotland next autumn.

Christopher has now reached the ripe old age of 27 and is working in the computer industry near London. He still orienteers regularly and, as a Level Two coach, helps with the local Regional Squad, but hasn't the leisure or nervous energy left after working in the city to spend the time on the levels of serious training needed to reach the top. As a junior he reached the National Junior Squad and ran well for England in the annual Junior Home International. He travelled to squad courses abroad and competed in major competitions like the Swedish, Swiss and Czech 5 Day events, but he never achieved the technical consistency to match his running speed, and remained an interesting rather than a regular top level performer. He still writes to Swedish penfriend Björn who is now a member of the Swedish team and was 10th in the last World Championship. After leaving university, Chris spent a year walking, and orienteering, in Australia and New Zealand. He made many friends and is shortly to be best man at an Australian friend's wedding. Life without running, forests and weekend breaks in the countryside is unimaginable .... He doesn't see himself settling down yet.

Fig 12.1: Reaching the top

Samantha has reached the top. Now 25, she is studying Ecology at a Swedish University. She is a regular member of the British Orienteering team and was 11th in the recent World Championships. She lives in a student hostel in central Sweden, has many friends in the world of sport, enjoys skiing in the snowy winters almost as much as orienteering and has orienteered in most of the International Orienteering Federation's 45 member countries.

She always trains in a very determined and organised way, builds a detailed year's programme round work and study, and returns to Britain regularly to run in major events and selection races. She is currently ranked No 2 in Britain and hopes to reach the top 10 in the world this year. When she has finished her studies she hopes to work in environmental research. Although her tightly organised life leaves little time for social events, she has a friend who is a cross-country skier. When the snow disappears, she loves back-packing with him in the northern fells in the spring sunshine, as with the rest of the family, orienteering has given her a wonderful key to the natural world.

Each Christmas, the Wood family still get together in the family home and swap stories and experiences of the year. A stream of orienteering friends call in, linked or cross-linked with different members of the family. The Christmas cards round the wall bear testimony to the breadth of the orienteering family which has embraced them all. For New Year they and friends will have a reunion at Rose Cottage above Tarn Hows in the Lake District where they will again run the Round the Tarn family handicap and relive happy training days in the past.

Orienteering had given the Wood family a lot, just as they have all ploughed back their experience into the sport. They could never have imagined the

Fig 12.2: Tarn Hows

complicated journey that their first permanent course experience of orienteering would open up for them. It has been a marvellous door to the natural world. While so much natural conservation in the 90's centres round survival strategies, orienteering's relationship with nature remains a living, dynamic one.

The Wood family experiences as described here are there to be tasted and shared - hopefully by you the reader. I have enjoyed providing a peep-hole into their lives and sharing my teaching and coaching experience with you. Every situation, exercise and idea described in this book is based on solid fact, including the map illustrations. There are many in the current British international and coaching scenes, and their families, who will identify with the family adventures

I have described. I am sure many orienteers from other countries will find echoes of their experience too.

But orienteering is not about lectures and seminars. It's about getting out there and doing it, and in the process, getting to grips with one's own fears and uncertainties. It's as much about knowing oneself and competing with self and the forest as it is about competition with others. So now get those orienteering shoes on and get out there amongst the trees and hills. Who knows where today's path may take you? Wherever it is, you'll taste experiences, thrills and challenges you never dreamt of at the start, and if orienteering brings to your lives half the pleasure it has brought to mine and my family's, then your journey will have been rich indeed.

Epilogue

My proof reading of 'Pathways to Excellence' followed closely upon an international course on orienteering development I had been running near Ornsköldsvik in Northern Sweden prior to the annual 5 Days O-Ringen competition.

Representatives from 15 nations spent 4 days discussing the development of family, club and schools' orienteering in their respective countries while son Stephen and I, with Carol McNeill, translated our British experience into practical exercises in the rock and marsh of local Swedish forests. The participants had many tales to tell which echoed the experiences of the Wood family in Britain and I append here some of my impressions of an inspiring occasion which brought home to me yet again what a superb catalyst the sport of orienteering is for shared enjoyment in the countryside.

For 5 days 15,000 men, women and children of all ages and abilities competed on a multitude of courses planned and organised by hundreds of unpaid volunteers from the Ornsköldsvik community. Every morning a continuous file of brightly attired competitors wound its way beside blue lakes, along aromatic forest paths and across fields edged with wild flowers to one of eight starts, while local residents waved greetings from their traditional copper red white-framed homes. Elite competitors in lycra tights with their colourful sponsor logos threaded their way through groups of chattering children and plodding middle-aged men and women while, with 35 nationalities represented, the languages were sometimes as varied as styles of dress and gait.

The start areas in sunlit forest glades were strangely silent. As a 'bleeper' sounded the count down to each minute, six or seven competitors stepped forward to a wooden gantry to pick up control card, descriptions and finally map, before slipping quietly into the natural arena of fire tree, bilberry and lichen-covered rock to find the elusive orange and white markers skillfully positioned on small wooden platforms beside boulders, knolls and marshes on their respective courses.

The vast Swedish forests mysteriously soak up the large numbers of competitors. There is little sound apart from panting breath and the rustle of undergrowth until, at the end of each course, runners cascade into a sunny meadow to stamp the last control and run down one of eight ribboned channels towards a finish gantry crowned with national flags and bunting. For 6 hours a continuous stream of humanity pours down the hillside to shouts of encouragement from club friends and supporters while the announcer gives significant results and interviews panting finishers in four different languages. Disabled competitors in wheelchairs share lane 8 with recreational competitors. Beyond the finish marquees, thirsty runners slake their thirst from drink points, look at the results boards and return to club groups congregated beside their banners or tents to share experiences and rest weary legs - then to the outdoor showers, refreshment kiosks or souvenir shops before journeying back the 20 minutes to the Event Centre in Ornsköldsvik.

Most competitors are staying with their clubs in 'O-Ringen City', a vast array of tents and caravans housing 20,000 people - complete with supermarket and sports shop marquees, banks, launderettes, showers, toilets, cafeterias and snack bars. Nothing is forgotten - even down to electric shaving points above washing bowls in an open field. For more than a week, orienteering becomes part of the local community and inevitibly, the streams of buses, bikes and walking groups commute to competitions, training events, swimming pools, lakeside barbecues and evening discos on a bewildering network of roads, tracks and pathways - many realigned for this special 100th anniversary week in the town's history - and all overlooked by a vast ski jump cantilevering out spectacularly from a rocky hillside.

As I walked the 2 kilometres to my start on Day 5 I saw many 'Woods'. Waiting for my start time to appear on the electronic display, I saw 'Natalies' sprinting along the path to the start triangle and 'Samanthas' carefully setting their maps before moving off steadily but confidently to their first control. As I struggled with map-to-ground and ground-to-map skills among the mossy boulders and marshes on rocky plateaus, I thought of Helen and Michael battling with the same techniques on their Lake District courses. Afterwards I chatted to a group of English youngsters on their first trip to Sweden. Tom, Duncan, Andrew and Steven had all experienced the same difficulties as Chris in keeping speed and technique in tune, all had lost many minutes at some controls trying to relocate. Lisa, like Natalie, told me of her efforts in mapping her school site back in Britain and with Louise, we talked of how they had involved their families in orienteering.

After each day's competition, I had discussed the course members' performances and they had described their routes on their courses with the help of an overhead projector. Marina and Olga from Russia found the forests very like their own in the Ural Mountains, Mikki Snell and husband Peter from Texas found the forests very difficult and Peter, in particular, as former Olympic Champion at 800 and 1500 metres had problems adjusting his speed to the difficulties of navigation. Osolya from Hungary, Michel from Austria and Brenda from Ireland also ran too fast but Jan's daughter Sophie from Belgium ran fast in the right direction on Day 3 and everyone shared her pleasure in winning a prize watch. We all listened intently to Steve after Day 1 as he explained how he had beaten the World Champion. Hugh from Australia, Mike from New Zealand and Chen from Israel were interested in how much help clubs provided in the UK.

Orienteering maps and courses provided a universal language and challenge which had transcended national boundaries and brought all of us together in a shared adventure experience.

So as I cross the last 't' and dot the 'i' I hope the mesage of this book evokes the same responses in you the reader as in me. I am certain now, if I ever needed convincing, that orienteering offers a Pathway to Excellence for everyone no matter what their nationality, age, sex or ability - truly, a sport for all.

Peter Palmer, July 23 1994.

Appendix A Types of orienteering course

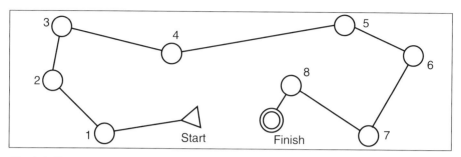

Fig. A.1: Cross country orienteering

In the basic competitive form of orienteering, cross country, a course is completed by visiting a number of control points in a set order. The winner is the person who correctly completes the course in the shortest time.

In score events a large number of controls are set out and each is given a points value. A set time is given to visit as many controls as

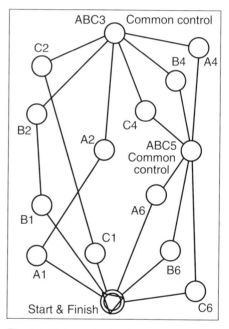

Fig. A.3: Relay orienteering

possible, with a scale of penalty points being deducted for late return.

Relays are fun and exert time pressure as well as team responsibility on competitors. Teams are normally of three with forking systems to reduce the possibility of competitors following each other. Common controls enable race progress to be judged.

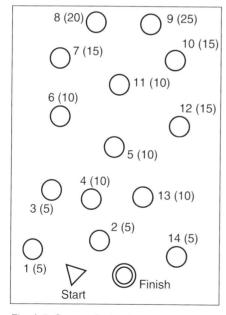

Fig. A.2: Score orienteering

Appendix B
Orienteering compasses

The compass is a direction finding instrument invaluable as an aid to precise navigation. Correct use will allow the orienteer to keep the map orientated in order to select routes and follow them faster while maintaining contact with the map. Maps used for orienteering have only magnetic north lines. This enables the compass to be used easily for map orientation.

Orienteers use four different types of compass:

Map Guide Compass
This is designed to help the beginner to concentrate on orientating and thumbing the map.

Silva Type 7DNS Direct Compass
This is a much simplified version of the standard protractor compas designed especially for children. It allows map orientation, direction checking and rough bearings to cut corners or aim off. It is also useful for beginners.

Protractor Compass
This type of compass can be used to take bearings as well as set the map. The protractor compass is the type most commonly used in competition. Considerable practice is required to use this compass accurately.

Thumb Compass
Like the protractor compass this type is used at all levels as a competition compass. It is carried on the thumb of the hand that holds

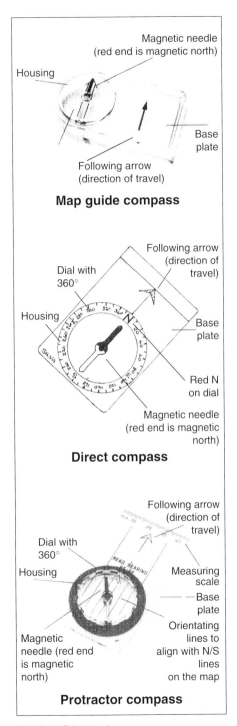

Map guide compass

Direct compass

Protractor compass

Fig. B.1: Orienteering compasses

the map, and the two are used as one unit. Some types of thumb compass include a rotatable housing so that accurate bearings can be taken. Others do not have this facility, allowing only map orientation and rough bearings.

It is important that whichever compass is chosen it is used in the correct way.

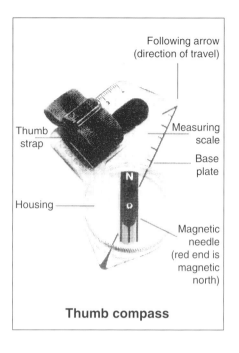

Following arrow (direction of travel)

Thumb strap

Measuring scale

Base plate

Housing

Magnetic needle (red end is magnetic north)

Thumb compass

Appendix C

International Control Description Symbols

Class	Course length in metres	Climbing in metres
H21E	12,300	· 270

A	B	C	D	E	F	G	H
5	49	⊞	◀		1.5	◯	◻

The most important items lie to the right of the thicker lines

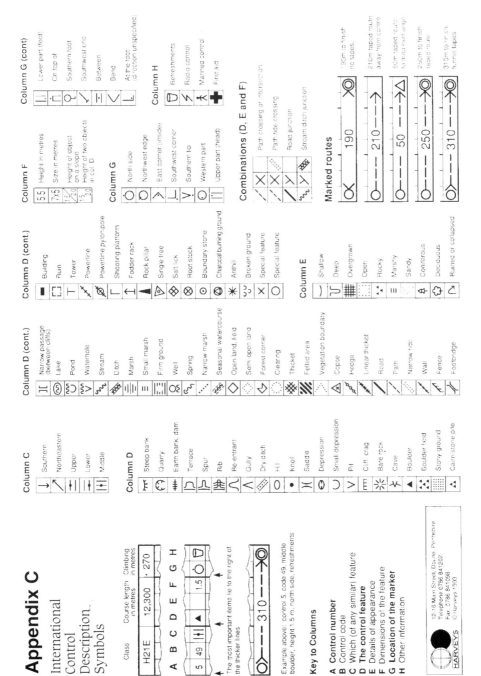

Example above: control 5, code 49, middle boulder, height 1.5 m, north side, refreshments

Key to Columns

A **Control number**
B Control code
C Which (of any similar) feature
D **The control feature**
E Details of appearance
F Dimensions of the feature
G **Location of the marker**
H Other information

Column C

	Southern
	Northeastern
	Upper
	Lower
	Middle

Column D

	Steep bank
	Quarry
	Earth bank, dam
	Terrace
	Spur
	Rib
	Re-entrant
	Gully
	Dry ditch
	Hill
	Knoll
	Saddle
	Depression
	Small depression
	Pit
	Cliff, crag
	Bare rock
	Cave
	Boulder
	Boulder field
	Stony ground
	Cairn, stone pile

Column D (cont.)

	Narrow passage (between cliffs)
	Lake
	Pond
	Waterhole
	Stream
	Ditch
	Marsh
	Small marsh
	Firm ground
	Well
	Spring
	Narrow marsh
	Seasonal watercourse
	Open land, field
	Semi-open land
	Forest corner
	Clearing
	Thicket
	Felled area
	Vegetation boundary
	Copse
	Hedge
	Linear thicket
	Road
	Path
	Narrow ride
	Wall
	Fence
	Footbridge

Column D (cont)

	Building
	Ruin
	Tower
	Powerline
	Powerline pylon, pole
	Shooting platform
	Fodder rack
	Rock pillar
	Single tree
	Salt lick
	Root stock
	Boundary stone
	Charcoal burning ground
	Anthill
	Broken ground
	Special feature
	Special feature

Column E

	Shallow
	Deep
	Overgrown
	Open
	Rocky
	Marshy
	Sandy
	Coniferous
	Deciduous
	Ruined or collapsed

Column F

5·5	Height in metres
7×5	Size in metres
	Height of object on a slope
	Height of two objects in col D

Column G

	North side
	Northwest edge
	East corner (inside)
	Southwest corner
	Southern tip
	Western part
	Upper part (head)

Column G (cont)

	Lower part (foot)
	On top of
	Southern foot
	Southwest end
	Between
	Bend
	At the foot (direction unspecified)

Column H

	Refreshments
	Radio control
	Manned control
	First aid

Combinations (D, E and F)

	Path crossing or intersection
	Path ride crossing
	Road junction
	Stream ditch junction

Marked routes

◯✕ 190	190m to finish no tapes
◯— 210 →	210m taped route away from control
◯- - 50 -◁	50m taped route to road crossing
◯- - 250 -✕	250m to finish taped route
◯- - 310 →	310m to control, tunnel tapes

HARVEYS
12-16 Main Street, Doune, Perthshire
Telephone 0786 841202
Fax 0786 841098
© Harveys 1993

Appendix D
The planning of orienteering courses

The shape and challenge of a cross country orienteering course, whether individual or relay, are defined by a series of navigational legs for which control markers act as turning points. A good course is more about navigating skilfully between controls than finding markers.

Planners try to give every competitor the experience he or she seeks from orienteering. This will vary according to age, sex, skill level and fitness and so every event offers a spectrum of courses with consistent technical and physical standards for each level and average times in line with nationally approved guidelines.

Handrail orienteering is offered to very young orienteers and *beginners* with a minimum of route choice and easy control points on or near line features like paths or fence boundaries. Time lost by mistakes can be limited by the use of catching features. Children mature at different ages just as veterans age in different stages. By planning courses to a skills progression and keeping coaching and competitive systems in tandem, competitors can move up or down a class as appropriate, and thereby still compete at their own level. *Ages 12 to 16* and 50 to 70 are the most difficult to cater for. Young girls in particular have difficulties in adjusting to physical changes which affect balance and speed.

Elite courses are demanding and test every orienteering skill - map and compass, route choice, contour visualisation, fine navigation and physical and mental strengths. Legs vary in length, change direction and extract the full potential from the terrain, thereby testingl competitor ability to match speed to the difficulty of a leg. The straighter the chosen route, the greater is the demand on navigational technique.

For *veteran competitors* over 40, planners try to keep a delicate balance between technical and physical demands. Steep climbs, long treks across rough or rocky areas, and areas of great map detail which fading eyesight finds difficult to read, are usually avoided In major events, clearer maps at a larger scale of 1:10000 are often provided for those over 45. Because there is often a wide gulf between the few fit veterans (e.g. early retired!) and the more philosophical recreational middle aged competitors, many competitions offer a choice of long or short courses.

Skilful course planning tries to provide some or all of the key experiences: Accurate Navigation, the Right Speed, the Exhilaration of Forest Running, Problem Solving, Exploration, Challenge and Adventure, Discovery, and Communion with Nature.

Planned and organised with sensitivity, orienteering can provide the supreme model for mixing man and the environment in mutually positive ways.

Appendix E

Specimen Summer Club Training Programme
12 Weekday Evenings

A progressive series of exercises, highlighting and reinforcing basic orienteering skills

Week 1   Handrail orienteering, following line features.

Week 2   Simplifying navigation, rough orienteering, catching features, check points, attack points.

Week 3   Line event, keeping contact.

Week 4   Control picking.

Week 5   Route choice; pairs compare alternative routes.

Week 6   Compass/pacing, flat area, blank map.

Week 7   Fine orienteering.

Week 8   Contour visualisation, contour only map.

Week 9   Relocation, pairs using one map.

Week 10   Window/corridor exercise, sections of map blanked out to reinforce compass/pacing and relocation near the control.

Week 11   Relay training, head-to-head race or clover-leaf loops in pairs/threes.

Week 12   Knock-out sprint orienteering competition followed by a barbecue.

If resources allow, an easy introductory course should be provided regularly for newcomers and children. A training area which includes a permanent course can help.

Club Weekend Training Camps can also be popular.

Make it Fun!   Make it Sociable!

Appendix F
Orienteering incentive schemes in Britain

Because orienteering is as much competition against self as against opponents, it is very much a self-motivating activity. Completing each course with a minimum of mistakes provides plenty of opportunities for progressive goals.

However incentive schemes can form an important part of learning and evaluation and five such schemes are described below.

The Step System
The British Orienteering Federation has developed a 5 level Schools Incentive Scheme based on the Skill Steps, (as shown in fig. 1.6, page 17), through which children can gain a badge and certificate for success at each stage as assessed by teacher or orienteering coach. Further details for this and the Badge Schemes below are available from the Director of Coaching, British Orienteering Federation (see appendix H).

Competition badge schemes
a) The Colour Coded Badge Schemes
The colour coded course guidelines appear in figure 5.1 on page 50.

A White Award can be made to anyone who completes three White courses.

The Colour Coded Standard for courses other than White is either the time that is achieved by at least 50% of those who started the course (including the retirals and disqualifications), or 150% of the winner's time - whichever gives the largest number of qualifiers. The Controller has discretion to extend the qualifying time, but not to reduce it.

A competitor qualifies for a colour award (other than White) by attaining the Colour Coded Standard for that course on three separate occasions.

Pairs can qualify for colour awards on the White, Yellow and Orange courses.

b) The BOF National Badge Scheme
This operates through pre-entry Badge and National Events which cover 15 age classes from 10 to 70 for both sexes and offer awards at

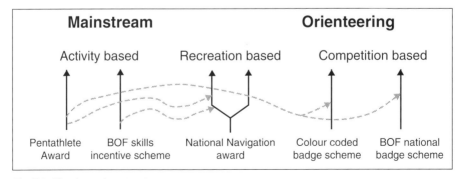

Fig F.1: The incentive structure

bronze, silver, gold and champion-ship levels for those who complete 3 events within a time based on the average of the first 3 in each class, i.e. gold = average time of the first three plus 25%, silver = average of first three plus 50%, bronze, plus100%. An iron badge is avail-able for those who simply complete three events regardless of time.

For children motivated towards excellence, consistent competitive success can lead to selection for Regional, Junior or National Squads which provide home and overseas coaching and courses. Many youngsters have climbed this ladder to achieve national and international recogni-tion, the ultimate incentive to raise personal performance levels.

The National Pentathlete award scheme

Orienteering features as one of 15 sports in this Butlin's sponsored incentive scheme run by the Central Council of Physical Recreation, Francis Street, London SW1P 1DE (Tel. 071 828 3163/4).

It is directed at 4 age groups (i) 5-7 years (ii) 8-11 years (iii) 12-14 years (iv) 15-16+ years. Young-sters can attain a bronze, silver, gold or platinum award when they achieve the appropriate level in 5 different sports within their own age group.

The orienteering activities were devised by BOF and include route planning, mapping and simple event organisation. Little equipment is needed, nor experience.

Schools wishing to operate the award contact the CCPR, who

issue a tutor's pack free of charge. This contains all details required to run the scheme. Successful partici-pants receive certificates signed by the Duke of Edinburgh and Gary Lineker for a small charge of £1 per student and tracksuit badges are available for a further charge.

The National Navigation award scheme

This is a new scheme which uses the orienteering method of naviga-tion as a basis for developing navigational competences in the wider world. It is aimed at people of all ages and abilities both in and outside the education sytstem, in fact anyone who seeks to explore the countryside with confidence.

A variety of outdoor centres operate the scheme within their training and 'taster' courses and, in the long term it is hoped that schools will take it up in a similar fashion to the Duke of Edinburgh Award, for older pupils 14-18.

The three levels centre on three basic levels of navigation as indicated below. Assessment will normally take place under the directionof a teacher or coach qualified through the BOF or Moun-tain Leadership Training Board award schemes. Further details are available from:
Administrator, National Navigation Award Scheme, 2 Greenway, Park Lane, Brocton, Stafford ST17 0TS. Tel. 0785 662915. or from BOF National Office, (see appendix H).

A school centred model

It is perfectly possible for individual clubs or schools to build up their own incentive schemes with internally produced certificates for successful candidates.

Pupils enter up each achievement in a log book or on an assessment sheet. The teacher signs to confirm each item and the final tally.

Certificates can be produced from internal school resources.

Schools can run schemes like this individually or as part of a group of schools in an association.

Activity	Points
Each training session attended	2
Each basic orienteering skill mastered	2
Each course completed, including permanent courses and closed school events	4
Introducing and helping a newcomer	2
Completion of an organisational task at an event	3
Surveying and drawing a simple map	10
Yellow badge	4
Orange badge	6
Bronze or red badge	8
Silver or green badge	10
Gold or blue badge	12

Fig F.2: Activity scoring system

	Boy/girl under 13	Boy/girl under 15	Boy/girl over 15
Gold award	20 points	25 points	30 points
Silver award	16 points	20 points	25 points
Bronze award	12 points	15 points	20 points

Fig F.3: Achievement totals

Appendix G
Glossary of common terms

Aiming off: To aim deliberately to a partricular side of a control on a line feature so that you know which way to turn on hitting the feature.

Attack point: An obvious feature near a control point from which the control can be reached by navigating carefully using map and compass.

Bearing: The direction of travel by compass; can be expressed in degrees.

BOF: British Orienteering Federation, Governing body for the UK.

Catching feature: An obvious feature beyond a control which will 'catch' you if you overshoot.

Cartography: The drawing of maps.

Col/saddle: Low point between two hills.

Coarse orienteering: Navigating by big features to travel rapidly, usually for the early part of a leg.

Colour coded system: A competition incentive scheme linked to a navigational skills progression. A series of colours represent degrees of technical and physical ability allowing competitors to progress up a competition ladder as their skills improve (see appendix F).

Contact (map): Keeping careful note of position while navigating by close attention to the map, using a compass as back-up.

Contour-only maps: Reprints or photocopies of the contour lines of a map, which show ground shape only, often used for training purposes.

Contouring: Keeping to the same height by running round a hill rather than over, to save unnecessary climbing.

Control feature: A clear feature on map and ground used as a control point on an orienteering or navigational course.

Control marker: A trapezoid orange and white marker used to indicate orienteering course control points, usually with clipper or punch attached to use to mark a control card as proof of visit.

D: Used to designate 'women' in international age class designations, e.g D50.

Description sheet: List of descriptions of the control features on an orienteering course, with codes for each control.

Fine orienteering: Precision navigation in detailed terrain demanding careful use of map, compass and distance judgement, usually over relatively short sections of a course.

Ground-to-map navigation: Noting ground features and then looking for them on the map as confirmation (the reverse of map-to-ground navigation).

H: Used to designate 'men' in international age class designations, e.g H21.

Knoll: Small hill.

Leg: Section of a course between two control points.

Legend or key: A list of the symbols represented on a map.

Line orienteering: Following on the ground a line drawn on the map. Used principally in training (see fig. 10.9, page 107).

M: Used to designate 'men' in age class designations, e.g M35.

Magnetic variation: The difference between Magnetic North (indicated by the compass) and Grid North (as shown on many maps), typically 5 1/2° west of Grid North in 1993.

Magnifier: Magnifying glass built into base plate of a compass or used independent of a compass to clarify map detail; particularly useful for middle-aged eyes.

Map case: Transparent plastic envelope to protect a map during a navigational exercise.

Map to ground navigation: Deciding navigational strategy from the map and then relating it to the ground to check progress.

Master maps: Used in some competitions and provided by the organiser. Competitors have to copy their course onto their own maps before the start of the competition or exercise.

Mountain marathon: A long distance navigational competition in mountainous terrain.

Orientating (setting or aligning) the map: Matching map to terrain so that north on the map aligns with north on the ground - the basic navigational skill.

Pace counting: A system of counting paces to check off distance covered over the ground.

Pace scale: A scale stuck to the leading edge of a compass giving distance in metres (or paces); used to check distances when running.

Parallel error: Mistaking location by fixing position on a similar and parallel feature to the correct one.

Permanent course: Orienteering course where permanent markers are set out in a forest or park area and overprinted maps are supplied. Usually used for recreation or training.

Photogrammetry: Drawing base maps from aerial photography.

Pre-marked map: A map with an overprinted competition course. Normally given to a competitor on the start line.

Pre start: A 'call-up' area usually 1-3 minutes before the actual start.

Re-entrant: Small valley or indentation in a hillside or the side of a ridge.

Relay: see appendix A.

Relocation: Finding oneself when lost, using a strategy of orientatated map, route memory and reference to obvious features on map and ground.

Ride: A linear break in the trees.

Route choice: A choice of route between control points taking into account difficulty, height loss and gain etc.

Runnability screen: See walk/fight forest below.

Safety bearing: A bearing given to all participants before a navigational exercise to indicate the most direct return strategy, e.g. due south (180°) to main road.

Scale: The ratio between a distance on the map and the same distance on the ground.

Score orienteering: see appendix A.

Sprint orienteering: Short distance competition in which pairs or groups compete against one another on opposed loops.

Step system: A progression of navigation skills starting with map familiarity at Level 1 and progressing to fine navigation at the top level. It can form the basis for coaching, competition or incentive schemes.

String course: A course for young children marked throughout by string or streamers so that children find controls without getting lost.

Stub: Tear-off portion of control card with competitor details and start time. The stub is handed in before the start of a navigation exercise or competition and used to monitor departure and return as a safety check. Stubs with finish times on are sometimes used as a results display.

Studs: Competition shoes with studded soles to give grip on rough terrain.

Terrace: A flat area on a sloping hillside.

Vegetation boundary: The boundary between two distinct types of vegetation, shown by a dotted line on an orienteering map.

W: Used to designate 'women' in age class designations, e.g W40.

Walk/fight forest: Green colour screens on orienteering maps indicate estimated speed of progress. The darker the green, the thicker the forest. 'Fight' means almost impenetrable.

Appendix H
Further reading

BOOKS ON SKILL DEVELOPMENT
The Coaching Collection
by Peter Palmer and Jim Martland (BOF)

Orienteering Technique Start to Finish
by Bertil Norman and Arne Yngstrom (IOF)

Skills of the Game - Orienteering
by Carol McNeill
(Crowood Press) 1986 ISBN 1 85223 5586

Organising orienteering
Guidelines for Course Planning
(IOF)

Orienteering for the Young
Carol McNeill, Peter Palmer, Tom Renfrew
(IOF) 1993

Orienteering Rules and Guidelines
(BOF) 1992

BOOKS FOR TEACHERS & COACHES
Orienteering in the National Curriculum
Carol McNeill, Jim Martland, Peter Palmer
(Harveys) 1992; ISBN 1 85137 0056

Key Stages 3 & 4 in the National Curriculum
by Carol McNeill and Peter Palmer
(Harveys) 1993; ISBN 1 85137 0102

Orienteering in the Scottish 5-14 Curriculum
Edited by Tom Renfrew and Drew Michie
(Harveys) 1994; ISBN 1 85137 0854

Teaching Orienteering
by Carol McNeill, Jean Ramsden, Tom Renfrew
(Harveys) 1987; ISBN 1 85137 020X

Start Orienteering
by Carol McNeill and Tom Renfrew
Series of 5 books for teachers (Harveys)

Developing Navigational Skills using the Silva Direct Compass
by Jim Martland and Sue Walsh
Coachwise NCF 1993; ISBN 0 94785 0902

MISCELLANEOUS BOOKS
Mountain Navigation for Runners
by Martin Bagness
(Misty Fell Books) 1993; ISBN 0 95210 0509

Trail Orienteering
by Anne Braggins
(Harveys) 1993; ISBN 1 85137 0900

Mapmaking for Orienteers
by Robin Harvey
(Harveys) 1991; ISBN 1 85137 0013

MAGAZINES ON ORIENTEERING
CompassSport
25 The Hermitage, Elliot Hill, London SE13 7EH Tel: 081 852 1457

Orienteering World
International Orienteering Federation
PO Box 76, S 191 21 Sollentuna, Sweden

Useful addresses

SUPPLIERS
Harveys
12-16 Main St, Doune FK16 6BJ, Perthshire
Fax: 0786 841098 Tel: 0786 841202
Orienteering books, teaching resources, equipment for organisers
• Free catalogue available

Ultrasport
4 St Mary's St, Newport, Shropshire TF10 7AB
Fax: 0952 825320 Tel: 0952 813918
Orienteering clothing, equipment, shoes

Silva UK
Unit 10, Sky Business Park, Eversley Way, Egham, Surrey TW20 8RF
Tel: 0784 471721
Orienteering equipment, clothing, Silva compasses, advice for teachers

Orienteering Services
Martin Bagness, 2 Gale Crescent, Lower Gale, Ambleside, Cumbria LA22 0BD
Tel: 05394 34184
Coaching and mapmaking

National Coaching Foundation
Coachwise Ltd, 114 Cardigan Road, Headingley, Leeds LS6 3BJ
Fax: 0532 319606 Tel: 0532 743889
Information, courses and resources for teachers and coaches
• Free catalogue on request

ORGANISATIONS
British Orienteering Federation
Riversdale, Dale Road North, Darley Dale, Matlock, Derbyshire DE4 2JB
Fax: 0629 733769 Tel: 0629 734042
Information on permanent courses, fixtures, clubs, courses and membership

International Orienteering Federation
PO Box 76, S 191 21 Sollentuna, Sweden
Fax: (46) 8 35 71 68
Information on international fixtures and rules, addresses of member federations

Appendix I
International (IOF) Map Symbols

contour	motorway, tunnel
index contour	major, minor road
form line	dirt road
steep earth slope	vehicle track
erosion gully: large, small	large path
earth wall: high, low	small path
knoll: large, small	intermittent path
depression: large, small	junction: distinct, indistinct
pit, broken ground	narrow ride
lake	wide ride
pond	railway
waterhole	major power line, pylon
uncrossable river, ford	small power line, pylon
watercourse: wide, narrow	stone wall, ruined wall
ditch, footbridge	high wall
uncrossable marsh	high fence, crossing point
marsh: open, wooded	fence, ruined fence
seasonal marsh	pipeline, uncrossable pipeline
narrow marsh	building, ruin
source, well	settlement
distinct vegetation change	permanent out-of-bounds
indistinct vegetation change	parking area, sports track
open land	firing range
open with scattered trees	high tower, small tower
rough open	grave, cairn/trig point
rough open, scattered trees	impassable cliff
undergrowth: slow run	small cliff
undergrowth: walk	cave, rocky pit
forest: run	boulder, boulder cluster
forest: slow run	large boulder, boulder field
forest: walk	stony ground, bare rock
forest: impenetrable	platform (non IOF symbol)
runnable in one direction	other features: vegetation
orchard, vineyard	land form, water, man-made

137